THE MESSAGE OF THE NEW TESTAMENT

THE MESSAGE OF THE
NEW TESTAMENT

F. F. Bruce

WILLIAM B. EERDMANS PUBLISHING COMPANY
GRAND RAPIDS, MICHIGAN

Wm. B. Eerdmans Publishing Co.
2140 Oak Industrial Drive NE, Grand Rapids, Michigan 49505
www.eerdmans.com

First published 1972 by Paternoster Press, Carlisle, Cumbria U.K.
Eerdmans edition published 1973
Printed in the United States of America

23 22 21 20 19 18 17   15 16 17 18 19 20 21

ISBN 978-0-8028-1525-5

TO THE MEMBERS

NORTH MIDLANDS

YOUNG PEOPLE'S

HOLIDAY CONFERENCE

Contents

PREFACE — 9

Prologue — 11

One
THIS MAN WAS THE SON OF GOD — 15

Two
IT IS GOD WHO JUSTIFIES — 23

Three
THE ETERNAL PURPOSE — 34

Four
GOD'S FIRM FOUNDATION STANDS — 43

Five
A FAITH FOR THE WORLD — 50

Six
JESUS CHRIST THE TEACHER — 62

Seven
UNCHANGING AND ONWARD-MOVING — 73

Eight
THIS IS THE VICTORY — 83

Nine
THE CHURCH IN THE WORLD — 89

Ten
THE WORD BECAME FLESH — 100

Epilogue — 112

BIBLIOGRAPHY — 117

INDEX — 118

Preface

THE JUSTIFICATION FOR PUTTING THE FOLLOWING CHAPTERS TO-
gether in this form lies in the call for a companion volume to
H. L. Ellison's *The Message of the Old Testament* in "The Christian
Student's Library". The "Christian student" for whom this series is
intended is a non-specialist, and for his sake I have tried not to
obtrude the common apparatus of critical study. It is hoped, however, that the individuality of the writers of the New Testament and
of their contributions to its message has been brought out.

A word of apology is due to other authors who have written books
bearing the same title as this, especially to my friend and colleague
Eric Hull, who wrote *The Message of the New Testament* for the
Religious Education Press "Understanding the Bible" series. And
more than a word of thanks is due to Miss Margaret Hogg for her
faultless typing of the whole work.

The dedication marks the conclusion of an association of nearly
thirty years with the North Midlands Young People's Holiday
Conference, at which I have on many occasions expounded various
parts of the New Testament message.

October, 1972   F.F.B.

Prologue

THE TITLE *The Message of the New Testament* PRESUPPOSES ONE question and begs another. The question presupposed is "What is the New Testament?" and the question begged is "Is there one New Testament message?"

What is the New Testament? To Christians it is the second and shorter division of their sacred scriptures, "God's Word written". The first and longer division, which they call the Old Testament, is also the Bible of the Jewish people. The designations given by Christians to the two divisions arise from the belief that the new covenant, foretold in Jer. 31: 31–34 as destined to supersede the earlier covenant which the God of Israel made with his people when he brought them out of Egypt in the days of Moses, has been realized in the new order inaugurated by Jesus Christ. This belief finds its warrant in Jesus' own words to his disciples at the Last Supper, when he spoke of his "covenant blood" about to be shed for many (Mark 14: 24). The books of the Old Testament, then, are those which record God's progressive revelation of himself under the old order; those of the New Testament record his definitive self-revelation in Christ.

Or, to put it in historical terms, the New Testament comprises all the writings which have any reasonable claim to be regarded as the foundation documents or primary sources of the Christian faith. They were written by about ten or twelve different authors within a century from the time of Jesus – some of the most important of them within a generation. Five of the twenty-seven (the four Gospels and the Acts of the Apostles) are in narrative form, twenty-one are letters, and one is an apocalypse – *the* Apocalypse, indeed, which has given its name to a whole class of literature.[1] The various authors did not write in collusion, although occasionally we can trace the dependence of one on another, as when the Gospels of Matthew

[1] See p. 83.

11

and Luke appear to draw on Mark's or a knowledge of the Pauline letters is indicated in II Peter 3: 15f. But they were written to meet a variety of actual situations in the area of early Christian life and witness. Not until the beginning of the second century was a start made with gathering them into one collection, and not until the second half of the fourth century do we find all twenty-seven books, no more and no less, listed as making up the New Testament canon.[2]

Is there one New Testament message? Have the respective messages of the various documents and authors a sufficiently significant common core to entitle us to speak of a single overall message? It is occasionally questioned whether they have. Some readers are so conscious of the diversity of viewpoint represented in the New Testament that they would say there are as many messages as there are authors. Others read the whole volume on one dead level and are unaware of any diversity at all. Diversity there is, but it is a diversity in unity. Even a very cursory acquaintance with the New Testament writings is sufficient to reveal that in their various ways they all bear consentient witness that Jesus Christ is Lord. To this extent, even at the outset, we can speak of the message of the New Testament.

If, then, in this sense at least we can speak of the message of the New Testament, how can it best be expounded? We might take up one aspect after another of the message and develop it thematically. Or we might endeavour first to penetrate behind the written documents and envisage the stages by which the content of the proclamation and teaching which they set forth took shape in the interval between the ministry of Jesus and the earliest surviving records, and then trace the fuller unfolding of their proclamation and teaching from the earliest to the latest records, adopting a "traditio-historical" method. What we shall try to do here is to take individual documents or groups of documents and consider first what the message of each is; then we shall be better-able to see in what way each makes its distinctive contribution to the overall message. The order will be roughly chronological, but not entirely so. The earliest dateable documents in the New Testament are the letters of Paul. The letters of Paul, however, presuppose some knowledge of the story of Jesus.

[2] A fuller treatment of this subject is given in my *Tradition Old and New* (The Paternoster Press, 1970), pp. 129ff.

Although none of our accounts of that story (the four Gospels) can be dated before the letters of Paul, it will be convenient to take the earliest of them – the Gospel of Mark – and examine its message first.

One

This Man was the Son of God

The Message of the Gospel of Mark

THE GOSPEL OF MARK OPENS WITH THE WORDS: "THE BEGINNING OF the gospel of Jesus Christ (the Son of God)". The "beginning" of the gospel is the record of John the Baptist's ministry, culminating in the baptism of Jesus and his forty days' testing in the wilderness (Mark 1: 1–13); the "gospel" itself is the whole story from Jesus' baptism to the announcement that "he has risen" (Mark 16: 6).

The background of this use of the word "gospel" or glad tidings (Gk. *euangelion*) is found in those chapters of the book of Isaiah which use this kind of language about the good news of Jerusalem's restoration after the Babylonian exile (e.g. Isa. 52: 7):

> How beautiful upon the mountains
>   are the feet of him who brings good tidings,
> who publishes peace, who brings good tidings of good,
>   who publishes salvation,
>   who says to Zion, "Your God reigns."

This whole section of the book of Isaiah, from chapter 40 onwards, provides the New Testament writers with an abundant source of Christian *testimonia*; the very passage just quoted is applied by Paul in Rom. 10: 15 to preachers of the gospel. Indeed, Mark is probably indebted to Paul for his distinctive use of the term "gospel". While Mark and Matthew use the word to refer to the message which Jesus preached, Mark is the only one of the four evangelists who describes the story of Jesus itself as "the gospel".

Mark and his Gospel

Modern study of the Gospels pays particular attention to the interplay of tradition and redaction. The nature of this interplay is specially evident in the Gospel of Mark. Mark did not write this work out of his own head: the story which he tells had been told by others for a generation before he set it down in writing. Ancient writers, from the early part of the second century onwards, inform us that Mark was Peter's companion and interpreter, and put on permanent record what Peter had been accustomed to relate in his preaching. Many modern scholars hold rather that the basic material in Mark's Gospel took shape not as the reminiscences of one apostolic preacher but in the life, worship and witness of the believing community as a whole. Perhaps both individual and communal factors were at work, but the point at the moment is that Mark inherited a body of information about Jesus which was not his own invention. This quite substantial element in his Gospel we call "tradition" – that which is handed down or "delivered" to someone else who "receives" it. We may compare Paul's language about parts of the gospel story with which he was acquainted: "I received from the Lord", he reminds his Corinthian converts, "what I also delivered to you" (I Cor. 11: 23), and again, "I delivered to you as of first importance what I also received" (I Cor. 15: 3).

But when Mark received the body of material which had been delivered to him, he organized it in a distinctive way. He was not content with transmitting to others what had been handed down to him; he was an independent author, not a mere compiler or even an editor. If we call the material which came into his hands the *tradition*, we refer to his own contribution as *redaction*.

The tradition as Mark received it did not consist only of isolated units – incidents from Jesus' life and teaching. Some of them had already been arranged in some order. The main outlines of the passion narrative, in particular, had been fixed for quite a long time. This narrative was related time and again in public preaching: Paul, for example, says that "Jesus Christ was publicly portrayed as crucified" before the eyes of the Galatians (Gal. 3: 1). It was repeated in every communion service: "as often as you eat this bread and drink the cup", Paul writes to the church in Corinth, "you proclaim the Lord's death until he comes" (I Cor. 11: 26) – and he probably means that the taking of the bread and the cup was accompanied by a spoken passion narrative, not just that it constituted in itself an acted proclamation of the passion.

But when we have said this about the passion narrative, we have accounted for a significant proportion of Mark's Gospel, for about one-third of his space is devoted to Jesus' last week in Jerusalem. Indeed, so disproportionate is the space given to the passion narrative in all four Gospels that one scholar described them, in somewhat exaggerated and frequently quoted terms, as "passion narratives with extended introductions".[1]

The Outline of the Ministry

The story which comes to a climax with a cross and an empty sepulchre at Jerusalem begins some miles to the east of that city, in the "wilderness" bordering on the Jordan, where John the Baptist carried out his ministry of repentance. John's baptismal ministry is for Mark, as we have seen, "the beginning of the gospel" (Mark 1: 1). After Jesus' baptism at John's hands and John's imprisonment, we move to Galilee, the scene of Jesus' own ministry (Mark 1: 14ff). We leave Galilee in Mark 10: 1 and follow Jesus on his way to Judaea through Peraea as far as Jericho; his entry into Jerusalem is recorded at the beginning of the following chapter. With this outline we may compare Luke's summary of Peter's preaching in the house of Cornelius (Acts 10: 36ff):

> You know the word . . . which was proclaimed throughout all Judaea, beginning from Galilee after the baptism which John preached: how God anointed Jesus of Nazareth with the Holy Spirit and with power; how he went about doing good and healing all that were oppressed by the devil, for God was with him. And we are witnesses to all that he did both in the country of the Jews and in Jerusalem. They put him to death by hanging him on a tree; but God raised him on the third day . . .

In this extract "Judaea" and "the country of the Jews" may refer to Palestine in general rather than to Judaea in the narrower sense, but

[1] Martin Kähler, *The So-Called Historical Jesus and the Historic Biblical Christ*, E.T. (Philadelphia, 1964), p. 80.

17

in any case the sequence is clear: first John's baptismal ministry, then Galilee, finally Jerusalem. And if the summary were filled out with illustrative material – as, in its spoken form, it certainly was – we should find something not unlike the Gospel of Mark taking shape before our eyes. When it is said that Jesus "went about doing good and healing all that were oppressed by the devil", incidents like those which marked his first sabbath day in Capernaum (Mark 1: 21–34) would come readily to mind to build up a vivid and memorable picture.

The Son of Man

The designation of Jesus as Son of God in Mark's opening sentence is not textually certain: a few ancient authorities omit the phrase.[2] His identity, however, is stated unambiguously by the voice from heaven which addressed him at his baptism, "You are my beloved Son . . ." (Mark 1: 11), and proclaims on the mountain of transfiguration: "This is my beloved Son; listen to him" (Mark 9: 7). But no human being speaks of him as Son of God before the passion narrative apart from the demon-possessed: demons might be presumed to have access to knowledge not otherwise readily available.[3] Throughout the ministry another title comes to the fore, and that on Jesus' own lips – the title "the Son of Man".[4] Mark assures his readers in advance that Jesus is indeed the Son of God, the one in whom God is perfectly revealed, but if it be asked what sort of person the Son of God is, Mark lets us see him in action and teaching, and brings out the significance of his character and mission by portraying him as the Son of Man.

The background of Jesus' use of the title "the Son of Man" is probably Dan. 7: 13f, where Daniel sees "one like a son of man" coming to the Ancient of Days "with the clouds of heaven" to receive from him everlasting and universal dominion. The kingdom of God which Jesus announced also finds its background here, but it is to his own words and deeds that we must look if we are to

[2] But the balance of evidence favours its retention, as in most recent English versions, e.g. RSV, NEB, TEV, Jerusalem Bible, New American Bible.
[3] Cf. Mark 3: 11; 5: 7 (also 1: 24).
[4] The first instances are in Mark 2: 10, 28; all the others come after the Caesarea Philippi incident of Mark 8: 27ff.

discover what he meant by the kingdom of God and the Son of Man. The kingdom of God takes its character from the God whose kingdom it is, the God whom Jesus addresses in the affectionate language of family life as "Abba, Father" (Mark 14: 36);[5] and this character is revealed in the Son of Man who is himself the embodiment of the kingdom of God.[6] As the Son of Man renders service to others instead of receiving it from them, so the kingdom of God is a kingdom in which the humblest service is the highest honour. When the Son of Man comes one day "in the glory of his Father with the holy angels", then it will be seen that the kingdom of God has "come with power" (Mark 8: 38–9: 1), but it cannot be unleashed with power until the Son of Man has endured his predestined suffering and death (Mark 8: 31, etc.).

When Peter, at Caesarea Philippi, hails Jesus as the Messiah,[7] Jesus takes steps to guard against any misunderstanding of this title in traditional terms of political independence and military conquest by telling his disciples immediately – and from then on repeatedly – of the impending passion and death of the Son of Man. They were not marching in the train of a warrior-Messiah who would at their head expel the Gentile oppressor; any would-be follower of his must be prepared, he said, to "deny himself and take up his cross" (Mark 8: 34). To "take up one's cross" was not a vaguely metaphorical expression in a subjugated land where the occupying power used crucifixion as a regular method of public execution.

The Passion and the Glory

The life-setting in which this Gospel was published was probably the Emperor Nero's attack on the Christians of Rome in the months following the devastation of that city by fire in A.D. 64. Shaken and near-demoralized by the suddenness and ferocity of this attack, they sorely needed to be reassured of the validity of their faith. What was better calculated to reassure them than this little book which sounded "a call to Christian loyalty and a challenge to a hostile

[5] Cf. p. 29.
[6] Origen sums this up when he designates Jesus the *autobasileia*, the "kingdom in person" (*Commentary on Matthew*, xiv, 7).
[7] Mark 8: 29.

19

world"?[8] If they had to suffer for Christ's sake, they were but following in the steps of their Lord, who himself had suffered at the hands of the Roman power. What he said about taking up the cross came home with power to them; nothing spoke more directly to their condition than his words: "whoever loses his life for my sake and the gospel's will save it" (Mark 8: 35). The recent persecution was to be regarded as no abnormal experience, but as something all of a piece with the heart of the gospel, which proclaimed that the suffering Son of Man was the ultimate revelation of God.

If, as has been said, one third of Mark's narrative, from the record of Jesus' arrival in Jerusalem (11: 1ff) onwards, is devoted to the happenings of the last week, the preceding ten chapters themselves contain repeated pointers to the suffering and death which form the climax of the Gospel. The controversial scenes of Mark 2: 1–3: 6 contain a hint of the coming day when the "bridegroom" will be "taken away" from his friends (2: 20), and end with a plot against Jesus' life (3: 6). The list of the twelve in Mark 3: 16–19 concludes with "Judas Iscariot, who betrayed him". The story of John the Baptist's imprisonment and execution (Mark 6: 17–29) implies danger for the new preacher in whom Herod Antipas thought he recognized John "raised from the dead"; and what is implicit in that story becomes explicit when Jesus, after descending from the mount of transfiguration, identifies John with the returning Elijah of Mal. 4: 5f, and says that as his enemies "did to him whatever they pleased, as it is written of him", so too it is "written of the Son of man, that he should suffer many things and be treated with contempt" (Mark 9: 12f).

This repeated emphasis on the Son of Man's fulfilling what is "written" of him points to some particular passage or passages of Hebrew scripture, and no such passage presents itself so readily as the Servant Song of Isa. 52: 13–53: 12. Here is one, called not indeed the Son of Man but the Servant of the Lord, who in obedience to God and for the blessing of men does suffer many things and is treated with contempt, and who by the patient endurance of humiliation and death crowns the service to which he has been called.

We are thus prepared for the passion narrative not only as the climax of the Gospel but as the consummation of Jesus' ministry.

[8] C. H. Dodd, *About the Gospels* (Cambridge, 1950), p. 2.

This is implied in his own words to the disciples about the nature of true greatness: "the Son of man also came not to be served but to serve, and to give his life as a ransom for many" (Mark 10: 45). These words echo the portrayal of the Servant who "makes himself an offering for sin" and thus "makes the many righteous" (Isa. 53: 10f).

If the Son of Man's passion is the consummation of his service to men, it also marks the fulness of his revelation of God and shows what is involved in his designation as the Son of God. When, at his trial before the high priest, Jesus is asked, "Are you the Messiah, the Son of the Blessed?" he gives an affirmative answer, but goes on to qualify it with words of his own choosing: "you will see the Son of man sitting at the right hand of Power, and coming with the clouds of heaven" (Mark 14: 61f). His claim to be *the Son of God*, that is to say, will be validated by the divine vindication of *the Son of Man*. And when the Son of Man, mocked, scourged and crucified, has breathed his last upon the cross, it is the Roman centurion in charge of the execution, the most unlikely man present (one would have thought), who proclaims the truth about his person: "Truly this man was the Son of God!" (Mark 15: 39).

At the same moment, says Mark, the temple veil "was torn in two, from top to bottom" (Mark 15: 38). Once the presence of God was hidden from men behind that veil which hung before his throne-room, the holy of holies, but now it is hidden no more. In the death of Jesus God has revealed himself to men in the infinite fulness of his grace. The torn veil and the centurion's confession declare the same message. The centurion unwittingly divulges what has been called "the messianic secret"[9] – a secret which (contrary to a widespread opinion) "is not concerned with the identity of the Messiah but with the nature of his task".[10]

Although Jesus himself had disclosed the nature of the messianic task openly enough, and invited his disciples to share it with him, it was not "until the Son of man was risen from the dead" that the truth began – gradually – to dawn upon them: the crucified Jesus is

[9] Primarily by William Wrede in *Das Messiasgeheimnis in den Evangelien* (Göttingen, 1901), E.T., *The Messianic Secret* (Cambridge and London, 1972).
[10] T. W. Manson, "Realized Eschatology and the Messianic Secret", *Studies in the Gospels*, ed. D. E. Nineham (Oxford, 1955), p. 220.

21

king, the way of the cross is the way of the kingdom, and those who follow the Son of Man in the way of the cross share his sufferings – and by the same token share his glory.

Two

It is God Who Justifies

The Message of the Earlier Pauline Letters

APART FROM THE FOUNDER OF CHRISTIANITY HIMSELF, NO MAN SO dominates the New Testament as Paul, apostle to the Gentiles. This is the designation he gives himself (Rom. 11: 13) and his right to it is beyond dispute, for it was he above all others who mediated to the non-Jewish world the message of Jesus. He began his active life as a member of the party of the Pharisees, a zealous champion of his ancestral traditions, and it was because he recognized in the movement launched by Jesus a mortal threat to those traditions that, by his own account, he "persecuted the church of God violently and tried to destroy it" (Gal. 1: 13). But when he suddenly received the "revelation of Jesus Christ" which checked his persecuting career, he received simultaneously the commission to "preach him among the Gentiles"[1] to which the remaining thirty years of his life were devoted.

His surviving letters come from the second half of his apostolic ministry: he had been a Christian for at least fifteen years when the earliest of them was penned. Thirteen letters in the New Testament are superscribed with his name, but their conventional arrangement bears but little relation to their chronological sequence. In the conventional sequence, letters addressed to churches precede letters addressed to individuals, and within each of these two categories the letters are arranged (with one minor exception)[2] in descending order of length.

Of the letters written during the main period of Paul's apostolic activity, before his last visit to Palestine, four – Galatians, I and II

[1] Gal. 1: 12, 16.
[2] Galatians, although slightly shorter than Ephesians, precedes it.

23

Corinthians, and Romans – are of outstanding importance, and are frequently known as the "capital epistles". It is on these that most attempts to systematize Paul's theology are based. His later letters contain further developments of his teaching, but it is to these four that we look for its foundations.

To the same period belong the two letters to the Thessalonians, shorter compositions which are the earliest specimens of Paul's extant correspondence (with the possible exception of Galatians).

Paul's letters are all "occasional" documents in the sense that each of them was addressed to a particular situation. None of them was written primarily as a systematic exposition of doctrine – not even that to the Romans, although it approaches more nearly to such an exposition than any of the others. This means that each letter emphasizes those elements in Paul's teaching that were specially relevant to its particular occasion; sometimes, indeed, this or that phase of his teaching may have acquired its form under the influence of the situation addressed.

Jesus and Paul

When we speak of Paul as mediating the message of Jesus to the Gentile world, the question is immediately raised whether Paul's teaching is a faithful representation of that message or a perversion of it. There is a superstition, widely held and fondly cherished, that the original teaching of Jesus, a message of sweetness and light, was transformed by Paul into a dark, rigid creed, imposed on his converts with fearful sanctions. It is a superstition, because it is maintained in the teeth of the evidence of Paul's own writings, which points to a very different conclusion.

There are, of course differences between Jesus and Paul. Paul was not the Messiah, the Son of God, the Saviour of the world. On the plane of human experience Jesus and Paul, while both Jews, differed in birth and upbringing, in education, in environment, in temperament, in idiom. As for temperament, Paul may beseech his Corinthian friends "by the meekness and gentleness of Christ" (II Cor. 10: 1), but these were not qualities which came to Paul naturally. As for idiom, we have only to compare the luminosity of Jesus' parabolic teaching with Paul's parable of the olive tree (Rom. 11: 17–24) or his allegory of Sarah and Hagar (Gal. 4: 21–31) to realize that Paul's strength lay in straight, unmetaphorical argument.

But they both shocked the guardians of Israel's law by the freedom with which they treated it and by their refusal to let godly people seek security before God in their own righteousness; they both made mortal enemies of the chief-priestly establishment in Jerusalem; they were both executed by the sentence of Roman courts. And, most important of all, Paul saw more clearly than most into the inwardness of Jesus' teaching as, following his example, he proclaimed a message of good news for the outsider.

Change of Perspective

If Jesus inaugurated his Galilaean ministry with the proclamation that the appointed time had fully come and the kingdom of God had drawn near,[3] Paul in similar vein tells the Galatian churches that "when the time had fully come, God sent forth his Son, born of woman, born under the law, so that we might receive adoption as sons" (Gal. 4: 4f). While the substance of both proclamations is the same, there is a change of perspective: the original Preacher has become the Preached One, for Good Friday and Easter have intervened. In Jesus' message and Paul's we have to distinguish not (as Martin Buber put it) "two types of faith"[4] but two different *ages* of faith.

The *form* of Jesus' Galilaean preaching, with its background of Daniel's vision of the kingdom of God and the Son of Man, would have been as unintelligible to the pagans of Corinth as Paul's preaching in Corinth would have been two decades earlier to the Galilaeans. But between the *essence* of Paul's preaching and that of Jesus' preaching there is no such gulf, when once we make allowance for the time-shift between the two.

While the kingdom of God drew near in Jesus' ministry, its advent "with power" (Mark 9: 1) lay in the future, although not in the remote future – it would be witnessed by some who heard Jesus speak. For Paul, that advent "with power" has taken place: Jesus

[3] Mark 1: 14f.
[4] Cf. Martin Buber, *Two Types of Faith*, E.T. (London, 1951), where the type of faith represented by Jesus and "central Pharisaism" is contrasted with that represented by early Christianity and Hellenistic Judaism.

has been "designated Son of God *with power*, according to the Spirit of holiness, by his resurrection from the dead" (Rom. 1: 4). The power which God put forth to raise Jesus from the dead is now at work in the followers of Jesus, conveyed to them by his indwelling Spirit (Rom. 8: 9–11); by that same Spirit the love of God, demonstrated supremely in the self-giving death of Jesus for his people's sins, is "poured out" into their hearts (Rom. 5: 5–8). The perspective has inevitably changed, because Jesus' death and resurrection, which were future events during his ministry in Palestine, are now past events, or rather parts of one past event, in which the saving work of God has been let loose upon the world. This was what the ancient prophets pointed forward to: to use the jargon of the schools, eschatology was in process of inauguration during Jesus' ministry; now that the saving events have been accomplished, eschatology has been inaugurated. What remains to be done before the consummation has mainly the nature of mopping-up operations after the decisive battle has been fought and won. Hostile forces, already disabled, have to be destroyed: "the last enemy to be destroyed is death", and with its destruction the resurrection age will be consummated, when God will be "all in all" (I Cor. 15: 25–28). But the blessings of that age are already enjoyed in anticipation by those who have been united by faith with the risen Lord: this is the work of the Spirit, whom they have received as the "guarantee" or "firstfruits" of the eternal glory which awaits them (II Cor. 5: 5; Rom. 8: 23). In inward experience they belong to the age to come, although in mortal body they continue to live in "this age". "Therefore, if any one is in Christ, he is a new creation: the old has passed away; behold, the new has come" (II Cor. 5: 17).

The change of perspective of which we are aware as we move from Jesus to Paul is a change for which Jesus' own words have prepared us. Absolutely, it is a change which can be dated in terms of world history, around A.D. 30; empirically, it is a change which takes place whenever a man or woman comes to be "in Christ" – to use one of Paul's most distinctive locutions.[5] When this change takes place in personal experience, one's whole outlook is revolutionized. "With us, therefore, worldly standards have ceased to count in our estimate of any man; even if once they counted in our understanding of

[5] See p. 38.

26

Christ, they do so now no longer" (II Cor. 5: 16). These words (quoted here in the NEB rendering) do not disown all interest in "the Jesus of history" in favour of the exalted Christ;[6] they mean rather that the believer's view of Christ is radically different from the unbeliever's, and that the believer's view of all mankind now takes its bearings from his view of Christ.

The Age of the Messiah

The letter to the Galatians was written in a spirit of white-hot urgency when news came to Paul that his Gentile converts in the churches of Galatia were being encouraged to amplify the gospel which they had heard from him by the addition of certain practices of the Jewish law – circumcision and the observance of special days. In Paul's eyes such practices were religiously indifferent, but an important issue was raised when they were imposed or accepted as matters of legal obligation. If those who so regarded them treated them as essential elements in the gospel, then the character of the gospel was changed. Paul's gospel proclaimed a salvation provided by God's grace in Christ and appropriated by men through faith: if in some degree salvation depended on the fulfilment of legal requirements, this was quite a different gospel – in fact, no gospel at all.

We cannot be sure how Paul had learned to envisage the future course of the ages when he attended the school of Gamaliel. Like all Pharisees, he looked forward to the resurrection age, but he was probably taught that "the age of the Messiah" (the period during which the coming king of David's line would reign) would intervene between the age then present and the resurrection age. The age then present was the age of law, inaugurated under Moses; one school of rabbinical thought held that, when the Messiah came, he would abrogate Moses' law, and this may have been Paul's view. If so, then Jesus (whom Paul, from his Damascus-road experience onwards, acknowledged as the Messiah) had put an end to the age of law. If, therefore, anyone tried to reimpose the requirements of the law as conditions apart from which God's salvation could not be enjoyed, this came perilously near saying that the age of law was still in being,

---

[6] This is the view expressed, e.g., by Rudolf Bultmann in *Faith and Understanding*, E.T., i (London, 1966), pp. 217, 241.

that the Messiah had not yet come, and that Jesus accordingly was not the Messiah. It was for this reason, probably, that Paul invoked an anathema on anyone who came preaching a gospel contrary to that which his converts had received:[7] such a "gospel" denied to Jesus the honour which was rightly his; indeed, it justified those who condemned and executed Jesus.

Reading between the lines of this letter, we may gather that, before Paul's conversion, the fact that Jesus died on a cross proved to him conclusively that Jesus was not the Messiah. The Messiah, almost by definition, was one upon whom the blessing of God rested in an unparalleled degree, whereas upon one who was crucified the curse of God expressly rested: "a hanged man is accursed by God", ran the ancient rule (Deut. 21: 23). A crucified Messiah was a sacrilegious contradiction in terms. But when Paul was convinced by irresistible evidence that the crucified Jesus was indeed the Messiah, now risen from the dead, this contradiction in terms had to be resolved otherwise. How it was resolved for Paul he makes clear in Gal. 3: 10–14. The law pronounces a curse on all who fail to keep it in its entirety: "Cursed be everyone who does not abide by all things written in the book of the law, and do them" (Deut. 27: 26). All who hope to gain God's favour by keeping the law are exposed to this curse, unless indeed they successfully "abide by all things written" therein. Failing such perfection, men in the age of law inevitably incurred this curse, and there was no means of escape from it. But now a way of escape has been provided: "Christ redeemed us from the curse of the law, having become a curse for us" – in other words, by taking on himself the curse pronounced upon "a hanged man" he neutralized the curse which his people had incurred by their failure to keep God's law. The redeeming benefits of his death were secured by his people when they placed their faith in him; but for those who still trusted in their law-keeping those benefits were not available.

Paul's insistence that salvation was to be had by faith in Christ and not by law-keeping was in line with precedent that antedated the promulgation of Moses' law. Abraham "believed God, and it was reckoned to him as righteousness" (Gal. 3: 6, quoting Gen. 15: 6);[8] those who, like Abraham, believe God are Abraham's spiritual

[7] Gal. 1: 6–9.
[8] Quoted also in Rom. 4: 3.

children and share in the blessing divinely associated with him and his offspring. The same principle of justifying faith recurs in the prophets: "he who through faith is righteous shall live" (Gal. 3: 11, quoting Hab. 2: 4).[9]

The age of law, in fact, was a temporary dispensation: the law served to bring home to men their inability to fulfil the will of God and left them no option but to embrace the way of release proclaimed in the gospel, "that what was promised to faith in Jesus Christ might be given to those who believe" (Gal. 3: 22).

Under the law the people of God were kept in the leading-strings of infancy; with the coming of the gospel they have attained their majority. Now they can enter into the good of their status in Christ as "sons of God, through faith" (Gal. 3: 25f). If the new age is the age of the Messiah, who now reigns from the place of exaltation to which God has raised him, it is also the age of the Spirit, who has come to dwell within believers and enable them to call God by the same affectionate term as Jesus used: "because you are sons, God has sent the Spirit of his Son into our hearts, crying, 'Abba! Father!'" (Gal. 4: 6).[10]

This new age endures until all the hostile forces in the universe have been subjugated beneath the feet of the enthroned Christ. The subjugation of death, the last of these forces, will coincide with the resurrection of the people of Christ to share the glory in which he will then be manifested. Thus will be launched the eternal age to come, in which God will be all in all (I Cor. 15: 24–28).

The Grace of God

Nowhere has Paul more fully entered into the heart of Jesus' teaching about God and man than in his insistence on justification by divine grace. For this is a principle which recurs repeatedly in Jesus' parables.

The actual word "justified" appears in the parable of the Pharisee and the tax-collector (Luke 18: 9–14); the tax-collector, acknowledging that he was a sinner and casting himself on God's mercy, "went down to his house justified rather than the other". The phrase "justified rather than the other" is not Luke's imitation of a Pauline

[9] Quoted also in Rom. 1: 17.
[10] Cf. Rom. 8: 14–17 (see also p. 19).

locution, for it reflects a Semitic idiom which is not present in Paul's formulations of the doctrine.[11] Jesus in these words described God's acceptance of the sinner in terms of the sinner's having been "justified", by way of an anticipation of his acquittal in the final judgment.

Again, the last-hired workmen in the parable of the labourers in the vineyard (Matt. 20: 1–16) do not bargain with the owner about their pay. If a denarius was the fair rate for a day's work, those who agreed at dawn to do a day's work for that sum had no cause to complain when they received it at sunset. Those who worked for the last hour only might have expected but a small fraction of that, but they accepted the owner's undertaking to give them "whatever is right" and in the event they also received a denarius each. "God's love", says T. W. Manson, "cannot be portioned out in quantities nicely adjusted to the merits of individuals. There is such a thing as the twelfth part of a denar. It was called a *pondion*. But there is no such thing as a twelfth part of the love of God."[12]

The same principle appears in the parable of the two debtors (Luke 7: 41–43): one owed a large sum and the other a small sum, but when they were equally unable to pay, the creditor, in the noble language of the AV, "frankly forgave them both". We see it again in the parable of the prodigal son (Luke 15: 11–32). When the black sheep of the family came home in disgrace and started off with the fair speech he had so carefully rehearsed, his father might have said, "That's all very well, young man; we have heard fine speeches before. Now you buckle to and work as you have said, and if it turns out that you mean what you say, we may let you work your passage. But first you must prove yourself; we can't just let bygones be bygones as though nothing had happened." Even that would have been generous; it might have done the young man a world of good, and the elder brother himself might have been content to let him be put on probation. And that is very much like some people's idea of God. But it was not Jesus' picture of God, nor was it Paul's.

For – and this is what Paul's doctrine of justification means – God does not treat men like that. He does not put them on probation to see how they will turn out – although, if he did so, that in itself would

[11] Cf. Joachim Jeremias, *The Parables of Jesus*, E.T. (London, 1954), pp. 112f; *New Testament Theology*, E.T., i (London, 1971), pp. 114, 117.
[12] *The Sayings of Jesus* (London, 1949), p. 220.

be an act of grace. But in that situation we could never be really satisfied that we had made the grade, that our performance was sufficiently creditable to win the divine approval at the last. Even if we did the best we could – and the trouble is, we do not always do that – how could we know that our best came within measurable distance of God's requirement? We might hope, but we could never be sure. But if God in sheer grace assures us of our acceptance in advance, and we gratefully embrace that assurance, then we can go on to do his will from the heart as our response of love, empowered by the Holy Spirit who is given to all believers, without always worrying about whether we are doing it adequately or not. In fact, we need have no illusions that to the end of the chapter we shall be anything more than unprofitable servants, but we know whom we have believed, and our confidence is in him. And how can such grace be accepted otherwise than in childlike trust, grateful faith? For Paul, as for Jesus, "religion is grace, and ethics is gratitude".[13]

The initiative in grace always rests with God. He bestows the reconciliation; we receive it (Rom. 5: 11). No matter what creeds, confessions and hymns may say about the need for God to be reconciled to man, for Paul, as for Jesus, God is the Reconciler. "God, who through Christ reconciled us to himself" (II Cor. 5: 18), no more needs to be himself reconciled in Paul's thought than the prodigal's father needed to be reconciled to his son. It was the son's heart, not the father's, that needed to undergo a change.

As God provides the reconciliation, so also he provides the redemption; we are its beneficiaries. The term "redemption" pictures man as enslaved to sin, viewed as a power from whose bondage man needs to be delivered. When Paul speaks of "the redemption that is in Christ Jesus" (Rom. 3: 24) he echoes the Gospel saying about the Son of Man who came "to give his life as a ransom for many" (Mark 10: 45). But if we ask to whom the redemption-price or ransom was paid, we find that we have overpressed the slavemarket figure; it has suddenly given way to the language of sacrifice, for it is to God, on behalf of mankind, that the Son of Man offers up his life "as a ransom for many".[14]

[13] *Letters of Thomas Erskine* (Edinburgh, 1877), p. 16, quoted by R. N. Flew, *Jesus and his Way* (London, 1963), p. 13.
[14] See p. 21.

31

Justification by Faith

What Paul has to say about justification by faith has been described as a "polemical doctrine" which he fashioned as a weapon with which to fight his opponents who were inculcating a message of salvation by the law among the churches which he had planted.[15] A fighting doctrine it certainly is – and a good doctrine to fight with, it may be added – but its place in Paul's thought is misrepresented when it is suggested that it was devised *ad hoc* in the heat of controversy or, in a different metaphor, that it is but a "subsidiary crater" in the Pauline volcano.[16] On the contrary, the essence of this doctrine is implicit in the logic of Paul's conversion. When the former Pharisee abandoned the law as the basis of his justification in God's sight, where did he find henceforth the basis of his justification if not in the crucified and risen Lord in whom he had come to believe? Although it was late in his apostolic career that he wrote of his ambition to "gain Christ and be found in him, not having a righteousness of my own, based on law, but that which is through faith in Christ" (Phil. 3: 8f), these words express his inmost attitude ever since the day of his conversion. And when he expounds his gospel in the letter to the Romans, in a situation free of the necessity for polemic, justification by faith occupies a cardinal place in his exposition.

The Freedom of the Spirit

Among all the New Testament writers, Paul is pre-eminent as the champion of freedom – freedom from every kind of spiritual bondage. But for him, the community of Jesus' disciples might have become another Jewish party – "the sect of the Nazarenes", as it is called in Acts 24: 5 – with its own variety of legal interpretation, distinguished mainly by its belief that Jesus was the Messiah.

Paul had been brought up to equate religion with law, but the day came when he discovered that law-keeping was not the way to peace with God. With his Damascus-road conversion came the assurance that his acceptance by God depended not on his own acts of righteousness but on God's grace, to be appropriated by faith. "Christ is the

[15] William Wrede, *Paul*, E.T. (London, 1907), p. 123; cf. apposite comments by Ernst Käsemann, *Perspectives on Paul*, E.T. (London, 1971), pp. 70ff.
[16] A. Schweitzer, *The Mysticism of Paul the Apostle*, E.T. (London, 1931), p. 225.

end of the law, that everyone who has faith may be justified" (Rom. 10: 4). And freedom in Christ meant not only freedom from law-keeping conceived as a means of justification before God, but freedom from the rules which some other Christian leaders thought necessary for the regulation of the life of new converts, especially converts from the Gentiles. In all things which were spiritually and ethically indifferent, such as food-regulations or the observance of special days, Paul taught that Christian freedom was limited only by considerations of Christian charity – and Christian charity could not be a matter of external dictation; it must be exercised spontaneously and voluntarily. It was by way of doing equal justice to the twin Pauline principles of Christian liberty and Christian charity that Luther began his treatise *On the Liberty of a Christian Man* with the two sentences: "A Christian man is a most free lord of all, subject to none. A Christian man is a most dutiful servant of all, subject to all." "Where the Spirit of the Lord is, there is freedom" (II Cor. 3: 17), but equally, where the Spirit of the Lord is, the love of God which he pours into believers' hearts will flow out to others. "The fruit of the Spirit is love", says Paul, together with "joy, peace, patience, kindness, goodness, faithfulness, gentleness, self-control" (Gal. 5: 22). No law can legislate for such qualities as these; they grow spontaneously in those who live by the Spirit.

The Spirit, moreover, is the Spirit of life. His indwelling presence in the believer is the pledge of resurrection and immortality. "If the Spirit of him who raised Jesus from the dead dwells in you, he who raised Christ Jesus from the dead will give life to your mortal bodies also through his Spirit who dwells in you" (Rom. 8: 11). Hence, though the outer man wastes away, the inner man is being renewed daily by that life-giving Spirit, until at last what is mortal is "swallowed up by life" (II Cor. 4: 16–5: 5).

Three

The Eternal Purpose

The Message of Colossians and Ephesians

THERE IS NO LACK OF INDICATION IN THE EARLIER PAULINE LETTERS that the person and work of Christ have cosmic implications. "For us", says Paul to the Corinthians (for us, that is, in contrast to pagans), "there is one God, the Father, from whom are all things and for whom we exist, and one Lord, Jesus Christ, through whom are all things and through whom we exist" (I Cor. 8: 6). If God the Father is the creator of the universe, Christ the Son is the agent through whom he created it. Christ, moreover, is "the power of God and the wisdom of God" (I Cor. 1: 24), and God through the Spirit has revealed to his people that long-hidden wisdom through ignorance of which the cosmic powers, "the rulers of this age", crucified the Lord of glory and so sealed their own doom (I Cor. 2: 6–10). And when the last hostile force is subjugated beneath the Saviour's feet, not only will his people be liberated from mortality but "the creation itself will be set free from its bondage to decay and obtain the glorious liberty of the children of God" (Rom. 8: 21).

The Cosmic Christ

The early Christian identification of Christ with the divine wisdom was particularly influential in fostering the conception of his cosmic rôle. In the Old Testament, creation is brought into being by the divine wisdom, and when that wisdom is personified (as it is here and there in the "wisdom literature") it becomes God's assessor, and indeed his agent, in his creative work.[1] Hence, when Christ came to

---

[1] Cf. especially Prov. 8: 22ff (see p. 104).

be recognized as the personal and incarnate wisdom of God, it was natural to recognize in him the one through whom, before his incarnation, God created all things.[2] This insight is not peculiar to Paul: it appears in the Gospel of John, in Hebrews and in Revelation[3] – a spread wide enough to suggest that it antedates them all and could have its origin in "wisdom-sayings" on the lips of Jesus himself.

In two of Paul's later letters – Colossians and Ephesians – the theme of the cosmic Christ is elaborated. The former of these was written to warn the Christians of Colossae and other cities of the Lycus valley in Phrygia against a prevalent form of teaching in which basically Jewish elements were amalgamated with the veneration of cosmic powers. These powers, which are called "the elemental spirits of the universe" (Col. 2: 8, 20),[4] meaning perhaps the lords of the planetary spheres, were identified with the angels through whom the law of Israel was believed to have been mediated (cf. Acts 7: 53; Gal. 3: 19; Heb. 2: 2). The keeping of the law was regarded as a tribute due to them; the breaking of the law incurred their displeasure and brought the law-breakers into debt and bondage to them. They had to be placated not only by traditional Jewish observances but also by rigorous asceticism.

This kind of teaching undoubtedly appealed to a certain religious temperament, the more so as it was presented as a form of advanced teaching for a spiritual élite. Christians were urged to go in for this higher wisdom, to explore the hidden mysteries by a series of successive initiations until they achieved perfection. Baptism was only a preliminary initiation; those who would pursue the path of truth farther must put off all material elements by means of a self-denying régime until they were transported from this palpable world of darkness into the spiritual realm of light, and thus had experienced full redemption.

But however attractive many might find this cult, Paul condemns it as specious make-believe. Far from constituting a more advanced grade of knowledge than that presented in the apostolic preaching, it was totally inconsistent with that preaching and threatened to overthrow the foundations of Christianity. A system which exalted

[2] Col. 1: 15–17.
[3] John 1: 1–3; Heb. 1: 2f; Rev. 3: 14.
[4] Cf. also Gal. 4: 3.

the planetary powers must enthrone fate in place of the will of God, and a system which brought men into bondage to these powers must deny the grace of God.

To this "human tradition", as he calls it (Col. 2: 8), Paul opposes the "tradition" which finds its source and authority in Christ. But in view of the cosmic emphasis in this "human tradition", it was necessary to develop the cosmic aspects of the true tradition.

The planetary powers have no part at all in the divine fulness; that fulness is completely embodied in Christ. It is in Christ, too, that all wisdom and knowledge are concentrated, and in him all wisdom and knowledge are accessible to believers – not only to a spiritual élite, but to all. The planetary powers are in no sense mediators between God and man; that rôle is filled by him who unites Godhead and manhood in his one person. He is not inferior to them; his sovereignty over them is established by twofold right. First, it was by him and for him that these powers were created, together with everything else that exists; secondly, it was he who vanquished them when they assaulted him on the cross, and liberated from their now impotent grasp those who formerly had been held in bondage by them. Why should those who were united with Christ think it necessary to appease powers which owed their very being to him? And why should those who by faith had died and risen with Christ, thus receiving a share in his victory, render any further service to those powers whom he had so completely conquered? Far from being an advanced stage of wisdom, this angel-cult bore all the marks of immaturity; it called on those who had come of age in Christ to go back to the apron-strings of infancy.[5]

The Body of Christ

In the earlier Pauline letters the church is more than once described under the figure of a body: "you are the body of Christ and individually members of it" (I Cor. 12: 27); "we, though many, are one body in Christ, and individually members one of another" (Rom. 12: 5). The figure is used principally to describe the interrelation of Christians in community, each performing his distinctive function for the well-being of the whole, like the various organs in a healthy body. The

[5] Col. 1: 16, 19; 2: 3, 8–15; 2: 16–3: 4.

unity thus set forth is symbolized in the Lord's Supper, in which the communicants participate sacramentally in the body of Christ: "we who are many are one body, for we all partake of the one bread" (I Cor. 10: 17). This consideration should be a safeguard against unworthy behaviour, such as idolatrous association outside the Christian fellowship or unbrotherly conduct within it: anyone who partakes of the Lord's Supper in an unbrotherly spirit incurs judgment, because he "eats and drinks without discerning the body" (I Cor. 11: 29). Similarly, fornication is out of the question for Christians because their bodies are "members of Christ": "shall I therefore take the members of Christ," Paul asks indignantly, "and make them members of a prostitute?" (I Cor. 6: 15).

But while in these earlier letters the body is the body of Christ and its members are members of Christ and members of one another, Christ himself is not integrated into the metaphor. A further stage in its development is found in Colossians and Ephesians: there Christ is the head of which the church is the body. In I Cor. 11: 3 Christ is called the "head" in another connexion: "the head of every man is Christ". There "head" probably means "source" or "origin", and the same sense may be present when Christ is called "the head of the body, the church" (Col. 1: 18; cf. Eph. 1: 22f); that is to say, Christ is the source of the church's life. It is from him, as the head, that "the whole body, nourished and knit together through its joints and ligaments, grows with a growth that is from God" (Col. 2: 19; cf. Eph. 4: 15f). Similarly, when Paul says in I Cor. 11: 3 that "woman's head is man", he probably had in mind the Genesis narrative of the formation of Eve from the body of her husband, who was thus the source of her life, and this analogy appears in Eph. 5: 23, "the husband is the head of the wife as Christ is the head of the church". We observe, by the way, that while in the earlier letters it is the local church in this or that city that is spoken of in these terms, the letters to the Colossians and the Ephesians envisage the church universal.

Naturally, when the relation between Christ and the church is presented in terms of the head and the *body*, a closer relationship is implied than, for example, when Christ is called "the head of every principality and power" (Col. 2: 10). The principalities and powers may owe their being to him, but they also owe their dethronement to him. With the members of his church, on the other hand, Christ is so closely and vitally linked that what is true of him can be predicated of them. In Paul's earliest letters they are said to be "in Christ"[6] and he is said to live in them; in baptism they have been "buried" with him, "united with him in a death like his" (Rom. 6: 4f). "But if we have died with Christ", Paul goes on, "we believe that we shall also live with him" (Rom. 6: 8), and we can anticipate our sharing in his resurrection by the living power of the indwelling Spirit. But in these later letters the people of Christ have not only died and been buried with him; in baptism they "were also raised with him through faith in the working of God, who raised him from the dead" (Col. 2: 12). They are exhorted to live as those who have died and been raised with him (Col. 2: 20; 3: 1), to "seek the things that are above, where Christ is, seated at the right hand of God", for the exalted Christ is their true life. It is but a short step from this to say, in the words of Eph. 2: 5f, that God not only "made us alive together with Christ . . . and raised us up with him", but also "made us to sit with him in the heavenly places". The hope of glory has been "realized" indeed, in the purpose of God and the ministry of the Spirit; but since it is realized in men and women still on earth in mortal bodies, it remains at present the *hope* of glory. It is in this sense that the Collect for Ascension Day bids us pray that, as Christ has "ascended into the heavens, so we may also in heart and mind thither ascend, and with him continually dwell".

Principalities and Powers

A Christian of the second century tells how in his pagan days he made the acquaintance of the Old Testament writings (in their Greek version) and how he found that these writings, read in the light of their Christian fulfilment, "put an end to the slavery that is in the world, rescuing us from many rulers, yes, from ten thousand tyrants".[7] He was describing that experience to which Paul points when he speaks of liberation from the "principalities and powers". These powers, whatever form they took, astrological or otherwise, enslaved the minds of men so long as men believed in them; to those who found release from their spiritual thraldom through the victory of Christ

[6] See p. 26.
[7] Tatian, *Address to the Greeks*, 29.

38

on the cross, they became impotent, "weak and beggarly elemental spirits" as Paul calls them in Gal. 4: 9.

Paul's language about "principalities and powers" or "elemental spirits" may have an archaic, pre-scientific sound today, although the current revival of astrology and magic suggests that a "pre-scientific" world-outlook is quite congenial to many of our contemporaries. But at a more serious level man today is unprecedentedly aware of powerful and malignant forces in the universe which he does not hesitate to call "demonic". He feels that they are operating against his welfare but that he is quite unable to master them, whether by individual strength or by united action. They may be manifestations of the "dynamism of history"; they may be Frankenstein monsters of his own creation; they may be subliminal horrors over which he has no conscious control; they may be aspects of the contemporary climate of opinion or current trends. He knows himself to be involved in situations from which his moral sense recoils – but what can he do about them? If he and his fellows are puppets in the hand of a blind and unfriendly fate, what difference does it make whether they resist and are crushed immediately or acquiesce and are crushed a little later?

To this mood of frustration and despair Paul still provides the answer. To be united to Christ by faith is to be liberated from the thraldom of demonic forces, to enjoy perfect freedom instead of being the playthings of fate.

Even if his terminology be thought archaic, his essential message is easily translated into the language of today. Whatever others might think, in his mind the "principalities and powers" were not the rulers of the planetary spheres; he has "demythologized" them to stand for all the forces in the universe opposed to God and man. Professor Rudolf Bultmann points out that "in our day and generation, although we no longer think mythologically, we often speak of demonic powers which rule history, corrupting political and social life. Such language," he continues, "is metaphorical, a figure of speech, but in it is expressed the knowledge, the insight, that the evil for which every man is responsible individually has nevertheless become a power which mysteriously enslaves every member of the human race."[8] It was this knowledge, this insight, that was present

[8] *Jesus Christ and Mythology*, E.T. (London, 1960), p. 21.

to Paul's mind when he spoke of the principalities and powers which were unable to separate believers "from the love of God in Christ Jesus our Lord" (Rom. 8: 39). More than that: the liberation which believers have already experienced will be experienced on a cosmic scale when God's eternal purpose attains its fruition and the universe is united "in Christ".

The Church in the Divine Purpose

In view of Paul's exposition of the cosmic rôle of Christ, and of the church's existence as the body of which he is the head, the question naturally arose of the church's relation to his cosmic rôle. What is her function in the universe over which Christ is exalted as Lord? What is her place in God's eternal purpose which is to be consummated in the Christ with whom she is so closely associated?

These are the questions to which an answer is supplied in the letter to the Ephesians, in which we are presented with a vision of the church as being not only God's masterpiece of reconciliation here and now, but also God's pilot scheme for the reconciled universe of the future. On the one hand, Jews and Gentiles who have been reconciled to God through the sacrifice of Christ have thereby been reconciled also to one another: "he is our peace, who has made us both one, and has broken down the dividing wall of hostility" (Eph. 2: 14). That dividing wall was the whole body of legal ordinances which partitioned off the Jewish community from the Gentile world, but which had been abrogated in Christ. The effect of his sacrifice was to "create in himself one new 'man' in place of the two" and to "reconcile us both to God in one body through the cross . . . for through him we both have access in one Spirit to the Father" (Eph. 2: 15–18). On the other hand, the removal of the Jewish-Gentile barrier carries with it the promise of the removal of other barriers which keep various parts of the human family apart. "For he has made known to us in all wisdom and insight the mystery of his will, according to his purpose which he set forth in Christ as a plan for the fulness of time, to unite all things in him, things in heaven and things on earth" (Eph. 1: 9f). All creation, and not merely the church, will come to acknowledge Christ as its true head and realize its unity and peace in him. Meanwhile, while this eternal purpose is working itself out, it is through the church that the "many-splendoured" wisdom of God is being "made known to the principalities and powers in the heavenly places" (Eph. 3: 10).

As Paul contemplated the unfolding of this plan, and considered the key part which his ministry to the Gentile world was playing in its fulfilment, he might well regard the trials and tribulations which beset him in the discharge of that ministry as negligible by comparison.

The vision unveiled in Ephesians has captivated other minds than Paul's. Samuel Taylor Coleridge, no mean judge of religious and literary worth, pronounced this letter "the divinest composition of man".[9] And a distinguished figure in the theological world of the twentieth century, John A. Mackay, has recorded this remarkable testimony:

> I can never forget that the reading of this Pauline letter, when I was a boy in my teens, exercised a more decisive influence upon my thought and imagination than was ever wrought upon me before or since by the perusal of any piece of literature. The romance of the part played by Jesus Christ in making my personal salvation possible and in mediating God's cosmic plan so set my spirit aflame that I laid aside in an ecstasy of delight Dumas' *The Count of Monte Cristo*, which I happened to be reading at the time. That was my encounter with the Cosmic Christ. The Christ who was and is became the passion of my life. I have to admit, without shame or reserve, that as a result of that encounter, I have been unable to think of my own life or the life of mankind or the life of the cosmos apart from Jesus Christ. He came to me and challenged me in the writings of St. Paul. I responded. The years that have followed have been but a footnote to that encounter.[10]

(It may be thought that Dr Mackay must have been a very exceptional teenager, but he was a Highland Scot, brought up to know what life's priorities were and to recognize excellence when he met it.)

---

[9] *Table Talk*, 25 May 1830; in H. N. Coleridge (ed.), *Specimens of the Table Talk of the late Samuel Taylor Coleridge* (London, 1835), p. 88. "The Epistle to the Ephesians", said Coleridge on that occasion, "is evidently a catholic epistle, addressed to the whole of what might be called St. Paul's diocese. . . . It embraces every doctrine of Christianity – first, those doctrines peculiar to Christianity, and then those precepts common to it with natural religion."

[10] *A Preface to Christian Theology* (London, 1942), p. 97.

If the church is to be an effective instrument in promoting the divine work of universal reconciliation, she must be seen to be the fellowship of the reconciled. She cannot convincingly proclaim the gospel of reconciliation to others if the barriers of creed, class, race or colour which are found in the world are tolerated within her own confines. If they are so tolerated, she has fallen into crass worldliness; her witness is nullified; the salt of the earth has lost its savour and has become good for nothing. Hence the second half of the letter to the Ephesians is largely devoted to practical direction to ensure that the purpose of God should not be frustrated by the daily life of Christians in the world.

Wisdom in a Mystery

In one of his earlier letters Paul told his converts in Corinth that, in spite of their fancied progress in wisdom, he had to feed them with milk instead of solid food because of their spiritual immaturity.[11] To those who were spiritually mature – and he measured such maturity in terms of growth in love as well as growth in knowledge – he had indeed higher wisdom to impart, "God's wisdom in a mystery", ordained before all ages for his people's glory, hidden from the cosmic powers but now revealed through the Spirit:

> What no eye has seen, nor ear heard,
> nor the heart of man conceived,
> what God has prepared for those who love him.[12]

If we ask where Paul imparts this "wisdom in a mystery" which the Corinthians were unable to take in, we need look no farther than the letters to the Colossians and the Ephesians. Here is the climax of Pauline theology.

[11] I Cor. 3: 1–3.
[12] I Cor. 2: 6–10 (see p. 34).

Four

God's Firm Foundation Stands

The Message of the Pastoral Letters

IN THE PREVIOUS CHAPTER IT WAS MENTIONED, ALMOST IN PASSING, that while the church in Paul's earlier letters is the local church in some particular place, in Colossians and especially in Ephesians it is the church universal. This development is a feature of what some New Testament scholars, especially in Germany, describe as "early catholicism". Other features are said to be the replacement of a charismatic by an institutional ministry, the recession of the imminent hope of glory at the Advent in favour of dependence on the present means of grace dispensed through the church and its ministry, and the adoption of a codified confession of faith.

Much of what is said about "early catholicism", with the implication that it was a deplorable declension from apostolic faith and practice, can be understood only in the light of the Lutheran tradition, and may almost be thought of as a reinterpretation of first-century developments in terms of sixteenth-century controversies. On this subject Bishop Stephen Neill has said: "A new and much more careful definition of the term ['early catholicism'] is needed, as also of the whole concept of 'authority' in the early Church. The results attained by such further studies will affect our judgment on the Pastoral Epistles"[1] (a designation commonly given, since the early eighteenth century, to the letters to Timothy and Titus).

[1] *The Interpretation of the New Testament* (Oxford, 1964), p. 344.

Church Order

The church is, on the one hand, God's "new creation by water and
the word", but on the other hand it is a community of ordinary men
and women who have this in common, that they have experienced
God's saving grace in Christ. As a community of men and women,
it needs in some degree to be organized and administered. The details
of church administration are mundane and humdrum indeed when
compared with the exposition of justification by faith or God's
eternal purpose; yet some place must be found for them if the church's
life and work are to be effective. Failing some provision for administration, any community faces the threat of anarchy, and when faced
with that threat men are apt to embrace dictatorship or even tyranny
as the lesser of two evils.

The Pauline collection of letters, then, includes these three short
manuals of church order, the prototypes of a genre which was
destined to multiply in the centuries immediately following. They
belong to a time when the Pentecostal flood waters of the church's
earliest days have receded and the stream now flows in a more clearly
demarcated channel.

So far as these letters are concerned, the church is not conceived
of as an institution for the dispensing of the means of grace, nor are
its ministers viewed as the agents through whom they are dispensed.
The church is pre-eminently "the church of the living God, the pillar
and bulwark of the truth" (I Tim. 3: 15); her main function, that is
to say, is to maintain the authentic gospel in the world, and the discharge of this function is the principal responsibility of her ministers.
Hence the qualifications of these ministers are carefully laid down,
together with further directions about the church's life, worship and
witness.

Yet, for all the detailed prescriptions for the establishment of a
regular ministry of elders (or bishops) and deacons in the churches,
the charismatic sanction of the ministry is not forgotten. Timothy's
own call to the ministry was marked by "the prophetic utterances
which pointed to you" (I Tim. 1: 18); the gift which he exercises was
imparted to him "by prophetic utterance when the elders laid their
hands upon you" (I Tim. 4: 14), and along with their hands Paul's
also were placed on him (II Tim. 1: 6). It was then that he received

44

the gift of the Spirit – the Spirit not of timidity but "of power and love and self-control" (II Tim. 1: 7).

If Timothy, then, is responsible to see that elders and deacons are instituted and recognized in the church or churches which he supervises, he has the guidance not only of the list of qualifications for these offices laid down in I Tim. 3: 2–13 but also of the Spirit whom he received at the inception of his ministry. Indirectly at least, then, it could be said of those instituted by Timothy, as it is said directly of the elders of Ephesus in Acts 20: 28 – and there is some affinity between Acts and the Pastorals – that the Holy Spirit had made them "guardians" (bishops) in the church.

Declension from Pauline Teaching

These letters presuppose a landslide away from Paul's teaching, especially in an area where one of the outstanding successes of his mission had been registered: "You are aware", he says to Timothy, "that all who are in Asia have turned away from me" (II Tim. 1: 15). They appear to have turned away in a direction which was both judaizing and gnosticizing: the leaders of this trend claimed "to be teachers of the law, without understanding either what they are saying or the things about which they make assertions" (I Tim. 1: 7); they taught an "over-realized" eschatology like their predecessors at Corinth, "holding that the resurrection is past already" (II Tim. 2: 18); they enjoined abstinence like their predecessors in the Lycus valley – abstinence (this time) from marriage as well as from"foods which God created to be received with thanksgiving by those who believe and know the truth" (I Tim. 4: 3). Once again the positions of saving truth and Christian liberty must be marked out, yet so that in recoiling from legalism believers do not fall into licence and "by rejecting conscience . . . make shipwreck of their faith". Timothy and others who would "wage the good warfare" must "hold faith and a good conscience" (I Tim. 1: 18f).

The Good Deposit and the Faithful Sayings

The future perspective lengthens: Christians are still encouraged to look for their "blessed hope, the appearing of the glory of our great God and Saviour Jesus Christ" (Tit. 2: 11), but as the time of the realization of this hope is unknown, provision must be made for the intervening generations. The torch must be handed on. "What you have heard from me before many witnesses", writes Paul to Timothy, "entrust to faithful men who will be able to teach others also" (II Timothy 2: 2). Here is an apostolic succession covering four generations – (1) the apostolic age, represented by Paul; (2) Timothy, Paul's disciple; (3) "faithful men"; (4) "others also" – but it is a succession of *teachers*. The body of teaching which is to be handed on is called "the good deposit". This "deposit" is identical with "the glorious gospel of the blessed God" with which Paul himself was entrusted (I Tim. 1: 11) and which he in turn entrusted to Timothy (I Tim. 1: 18). Timothy is charged to guard it (I Tim. 6: 20; II Tim. 1: 14), that he also may commit it intact to his successors.

The "deposit" includes precepts of Christian practice as well as statements of Christian doctrine; in fact, it covers the same wide range as the "traditions" do in the earlier Pauline letters (cf. I Cor. 11: 2; II Thess. 2: 15).[2] Some of the elements in the "deposit" seem to be pin-pointed under the caption "This is a faithful (sure) saying." Four or five times this caption appears in the Pastoral Letters, but sometimes it is not clear whether it refers to the words that follow or the words that precede it.

Happily, no doubt arises with regard to its first occurrence, a reaffirmation of the basic fact of the gospel: "The saying is sure and worthy of full acceptance, that Christ Jesus came into the world to save sinners" (I Tim. 1: 15). Such a saying could well have played a part in catechetical instruction, answering as it does three questions: Who came? Where did he come? Why did he come?

A double ambiguity besets the second occurrence (I Tim. 3: 1a): partly contextual, partly textual. Is the saying the enigmatic statement of I Tim. 2: 15, "Yet woman will be saved through bearing children, if she continues in faith and love and holiness, with modesty"? Or is it the statement that follows: "If any one aspires to the office of a bishop, he desires a noble task"? There is nothing enigmatic about this latter statement, but it might be thought too matter-of-fact to be introduced as a "faithful saying". There is, however, a variant

[2] Cf. F. F. Bruce, *Tradition Old and New* (The Paternoster Press, 1970), pp. 29–38.

reading which substitutes "human" for "faithful" and is well rendered in the NEB: "There is a popular saying, 'To aspire to leadership is an honourable ambition'." The implication may then be that what is honourable in general life is doubly honourable in the church, if the right conditions are present.

In I Tim. 4:9 the ampler wording of the first occurrence is repeated: "The saying is sure and worthy of full acceptance". It is debated again whether the reference is to the preceding words about the superiority of godliness over bodily exercise (because godliness is of value not only for this life but also for the life to come) or to the following words:

> For to this end we toil and strive,
> because we have our hope set on the living God,
> who is the Saviour of all men,
> especially of those who believe.

The poetical quality of these last words speaks for the higher probability that they constitute the sure saying. The initial conjunction "for" does not speak against this: it may appear intrusive in the present context, but is easily explained as part of the quotation in its original context.

The "faithful saying" of II Tim. 2:11 is also poetical in form: "The saying is sure:

> 'If we have died with him, we shall also live with him;
> if we endure, we shall also reign with him;
> if we deny him, he also will deny us;
> if we are faithless, he remains faithful' –

for he cannot deny himself." This is a call to faithful endurance, expressing the theme "No cross, no crown"; it catches up such Pauline passages as Rom. 6:8 and 8:17 and the saying of Jesus which we know from Mark 8:38 or Luke 12:9.

The occurrence of the caption in Titus 3:8 almost certainly has reference to the words which precede it, a remarkably comprehensive summary of the Pauline gospel: "But when the goodness and loving kindness of God our Saviour appeared, he saved us, not because of deeds done by us in righteousness, but in virtue of his own mercy, by the washing of regeneration[3] and renewal in the Holy Spirit, which he poured out upon us richly through Jesus Christ our Saviour, so that we might be justified by his grace and become heirs in hope of eternal life. Faithful is the saying."

Credal Affirmations

Other passages in the Pastoral Letters, while not called "faithful sayings", give the impression of being quotations from early credal affirmations or liturgical ascriptions. Among the former we may think of a further gospel summary in I Tim. 2: 5f: "For there is one God, and there is one mediator between God and men, the man Christ Jesus, who gave himself a ransom for all,[4] the testimony to which was borne at the proper time." Among the latter may be mentioned I Tim. 1: 17 ("to the King of ages, immortal, invisible, the only God, be honour and glory for ever and ever. Amen") and 6: 15f (". . . the blessed and only Sovereign, the King of kings and Lord of lords, who alone has immortality and dwells in unapproachable light, whom no man has ever seen or can see. To him be honour and eternal dominion. Amen").

More impressive still is the hymnic fragment in I Tim. 3: 16: "Great indeed, we confess, is the mystery of our religion:

> He was manifested in the flesh,
> vindicated in the Spirit,
> seen by angels,
> preached among the nations,
> believed on in the world,
> taken up in glory."

It has recently been argued, with considerable probability, that an early Christian hymn, originating in some such group as those Hellenists who first evangelized Gentiles in Antioch, and celebrating the triumph of Christ and the progress of the gospel, has here been

---

[3] "Regeneration" (here occurring in a quotation) is not a Pauline word, but it has much the same sense as the "newness of life" into which baptism leads in Rom. 6: 4; compare the "washing of water with the word" by means of which Christ cleanses the church in Eph. 5: 26.

[4] "A ransom for all" may be a re-wording of "a ransom for many" in Mark 10: 45 (see p. 21); the two expressions are synonymous.

adapted to a later situation. "The stress on incarnation, which originated in the Jewish idea of theophany, now counteracts gnostic doceticism and asceticism. The stress on universalism, which originated in the persecuted Christians' feeling of vindication by means of divinely ordered success in evangelism, now contradicts gnostic esotericism."[5]

The Sacred Writings

Behind the authority of the faithful sayings and other confessional affirmations stands the authority of the sacred writings which provided instruction in the way of "salvation through faith in Christ Jesus" (II Tim. 3: 15). These, being divinely inspired, are profitable for all aspects of Christian ministry; in J. B. Phillips' paraphrase, they "are the comprehensive equipment of the man of God, and fit him fully for all branches of his work" (II Tim. 3: 16f). The "public reading of scripture" was high on Timothy's list of duties (I Tim. 4: 13). It is the books of the Old Testament that are in view, of course; they constituted the Bible of the early church until well into the second century, and indeed in the second century the reading of them led a surprising number of educated pagans to the Christian faith.[6] But already in the Pastoral Letters we begin to see how the sayings of Jesus are given a status alongside the Old Testament writings: "The scripture says, 'You shall not muzzle an ox when it is treading out the grain', and, 'The labourer deserves his wages'" (I Tim. 5: 18). Here the prescription of Deut. 25: 4 (already quoted by Paul in the same sense in I Cor. 9: 9) is conjoined with the saying of Jesus which has been preserved for us in Luke 10: 7. In such a conjunction we may recognize New Testament precedent for the status given in the church to the two volumes of Christian scripture as constituting together her rule of belief and life. Here she finds herself established on "God's firm foundation" with its twofold seal: "The Lord knows those who are his" and "Let every one who names the name of the Lord depart from iniquity" (II Tim. 2: 19).

[5] R. H. Gundry, "The Form, Background and Meaning of the Hymn quoted in I Timothy 3: 16", in *Apostolic History and the Gospel*, ed. W. W. Gasque and R. P. Martin (The Paternoster Press, 1970), pp. 203ff, especially p. 222.
[6] Tatian (see p. 38) is an outstanding example; his teacher Justin Martyr is another.

Five

A Faith for the World

The Message of Luke and Acts

THERE ARE TWO OUTSTANDING HISTORIANS OF EARLY CHRISTIANITY.
One of these was Eusebius, bishop of Caesarea in Palestine, at
the time of the Council of Nicaea (A.D. 325), who wrote in ten books
a *History of the Christian Church* from its beginnings to his own day.
He had one predecessor, one only – the man who wrote the two New
Testament documents which we call the Gospel of Luke and the
Acts of the Apostles. Without further argument, we shall for our
present purpose follow tradition and call this man Luke. Between
him and Eusebius, two and a half centuries later, there are many
Christian writers who provide us with the raw material of historical
research, but none whom we can call a historian.

Luke's two books originally formed Part I and Part II of a history
of Christian origins. They were separated in the process of New
Testament canon-making early in the second century, when Part I
was incorporated in the fourfold Gospel and Part II pursued another
course. But they were written in the last third of the first Christian
century to provide a connected, if selective, account of events from
the closing years of the pre-Christian era to the early sixties A.D.

The purpose for which the work was produced is stated in the
prologue (Luke 1: 1–4), which was probably designed to introduce
both parts:

> Inasmuch as many have undertaken to compile a narrative of the
> things which have been accomplished among us, just as they were
> delivered to us by those who from the beginning were eyewitnesses
> and ministers of the word, it seemed good to me also, having followed
> all things closely for some time past, to write an orderly account for

you, most excellent Theophilus, that you may know the truth con-
cerning the things of which you have been informed.

Who Theophilus was – he is addressed again in the opening words
of Part II – we do not know.[1] He evidently had some acquaintance
with the story of Jesus and its sequel, but Luke writes to supply him
with a more consecutive and accurate narrative than he had pre-
viously had access to. He may well have been a representative of a
wider public which, Luke had reason to believe, would welcome such
a narrative. If we wish to have a more complete picture of this wider
public, our safest course is to read the narrative with care and consider
what kind of public the author of such a narrative would have had
in view. If in some measure his work is an account of Christian
origins for well-disposed outsiders, it is in more substantial measure
an exposition of the Christian message for those already within the
fellowship.

That the work was conceived as a history is clear. The earliest
incidents – those attending the birth first of John the Baptist and
then of Jesus – are dated "in the days of Herod, king of Judaea"
(Luke 1: 5) and with reference to the "decree" which "went out from
Caesar Augustus that all the world should be enrolled" (Luke 2: 1).
The public ministry of John, which was a curtain-raiser for the public
ministry of Jesus (the main subject of Part I), is introduced with an
elaborate synchronism, after the manner of classical historians, in
which "the fifteenth year of the reign of Tiberius Caesar" is corre-
lated with the tenure by a number of other persons of important
public positions in and around Palestine (Luke 3: 1f). The whole
course of Christian beginnings is set in the context of contemporary
world history. Not only is Luke the only New Testament writer who
so much as mentions a Roman emperor by name; his record, especially in Part II, makes repeated reference to governors and other
officials in the provinces and cities of the eastern Roman Empire
throughout the period which he covers. The faithfulness of his
narrative in this regard to its "dramatic date" (i.e. the date of the
events which it relates) has become almost proverbial.

[1] His title "most excellent", if used precisely, would mark him out as a member
of the equestrian order in Roman society; but it could be used more generally
as a courtesy title. It is given to the procurators Felix and Festus in Acts 23: 26;
24: 2; 26: 25.

The Defence of the Faith

The gospel started out, after the death and resurrection of Jesus, under what must have seemed to be an insuperable handicap – the fact that Jesus, whom the apostles and others proclaimed as Messiah, Saviour and Lord, had suffered crucifixion by sentence of a Roman magistrate. To Jews, as we have seen already,[2] the bare fact of his crucifixion proved that, far from being the Messiah, he died under the curse of God. To Greeks the idea of a crucified teacher and deliverer was just absurd, an affront to intelligent men. (And the assertion that the crucified Jesus had risen from the dead aggravated the affront.)[3] As for the representatives of Roman power, the movement was politically suspect in their eyes because of the undeniable fact that its Founder had been executed on a charge of sedition against Caesar.

The stumbling-block which the proclamation of Christ crucified inevitably presented to the different kinds of audience which heard it was dealt with by the early Christians in a variety of ways. The second century A.D. was the great age of the Christian apologists, whose writings defended their faith against attacks from Jewish rabbis, Greek philosophers and Roman magistrates. But these apologists have a prototype in the first century in Luke, in whose twofold history Christianity is defended over against Jews, Greeks and Romans. Its defence against Jews and Greeks takes the form of speeches uttered by outstanding figures in Luke's narrative; its defence against the Romans inheres in the course of the narrative itself.

Stephen before the Sanhedrin

Stephen's speech in Acts 7: 2–53 is traditionally called "Stephen's apology" or defence. In form it is a forensic defence, delivered by Stephen when he stood before the Sanhedrin on a charge of blasphemy; in content it is a defence of Christianity against Judaism. The blasphemy with which Stephen was charged arose out of his alleged claim that the new age introduced by Jesus marked the end of

[2] See p. 28.
[3] Cf. Acts 17: 32 (see p. 54).

the Mosaic economy and in particular of the Jerusalem temple-order and everything associated with it.

Far from denying the charge brought against him Stephen defended his teaching by an appeal to Old Testament history. The Jerusalem temple, he asserted, was not of the essence of true religion; on the contrary, it might foster false ideas of God by suggesting that his presence was tied in a special way to one place. But God had manifested his presence to Abraham in Mesopotamia, to Joseph in Egypt, to Moses in the wilderness of Sinai – all outside the frontiers of the holy land. The ancestors of Israel in the wilderness had everything that was necessary for the true worship of God; the mobile tent-shrine which housed the ark of the covenant was a more suitable sanctuary for a pilgrim people – as the people of God had always been intended to be – than a fixed structure of stone and lime such as Solomon had built. Their own prophets had warned them against imagining that the God of heaven and earth could be accommodated in a material dwelling.[4]

It is no accident that the Stephen episode forms the preamble to Luke's account of the origins of the Gentile mission. Once again God was calling his people to leave the fancied security of the traditional cultus and go out, like Abraham, wherever he might lead them. The danger was that, like their forefathers in the wilderness, they might look back instead of going forward.

Stephen's speech may be regarded as a manifesto of that circle of Hellenistic Jewish Christians who, in the sequel to his execution, launched the Gentile mission in Syrian Antioch and elsewhere. Echoes of it are heard in the next generation in the Letter to the Hebrews[5] and a generation later still in the "Letter of Barnabas".[6] But the position defended by this form of apologetic, that the new order

[4] Yet the temple is honoured in Luke-Acts as a place of prayer and worship. The first scene in Luke's history is enacted in the sanctuary (Luke 1: 8–23); the Gospel ends with the apostles spending the interval between Easter and Pentecost "continually in the temple blessing God" (Luke 24: 52). After Pentecost they continue to frequent the temple for prayer and preaching (Acts 3: 1ff, 5: 12ff), and Paul worships there when he visits Jerusalem from time to time in the course of his apostolic ministry (Acts 21: 26; 22: 17).

[5] See pp. 73ff.

[6] One of the writings of the "Apostolic Fathers", composed perhaps between A.D. 90 and 100, in which it is argued that the Jews went astray in putting a literal instead of a spiritual interpretation on the ritual and ceremonial laws of the Pentateuch.

inaugurated by Jesus has superseded the old Jewish order and represents the fulfilment of the law and the prophets, is a commonplace throughout the New Testament.

Paul before the Areopagus

The outstanding instance of the defence of Christianity against the Greeks is Paul's address to the Athenian court of the Areopagus in Acts 17: 22–31. This address, which found its text in an altar-inscription "To the (an) unknown God", is in essence a declaration about the true knowledge of God. God is the Creator and Lord of the universe, he does not inhabit man-made shrines, he stands in no need of service from those whom he has created, since it is he who gives to them all "life and breath and everything". The Creator of all things in general is the Creator of man in particular. Man is one, descended from a common ancestor; his earthly abode and the course of the seasons have been divinely designed for his benefit, in order that he might seek and find the true God. The true God is not remote and inaccessible; "he is not far from each of us" – and this assurance is reinforced by quotations from two Greek poets: "In him we live and move and have our being" (Epimenides)[7] and "We are indeed his offspring" (Aratus).[8] How foolish, then, to think that the true God could be represented by statues of metal or marble! To those who envisaged him by such means he was indeed an "unknown God". Thus far he had borne with men's failure to know him aright, but now a new situation had arisen. God the Creator of all is also God the Judge of all. The day of judgment had been fixed, and there was consequently an urgent call to men to exchange their false ideas of God for worthy ones – the more so as God had already appointed the man through whom this judgment was to be executed, "and of this he has given assurance to all men by raising him from the dead" (17: 31). It is only these last words, pointing to the recent resurrection of Jesus and his designation as judge of the living and the dead (cf. Acts 10: 42), that impart a distinctively Christian note

---

[7] A Cretan poet, reputedly of the 6th century B.C., who is quoted also in Titus 1: 12.

[8] A Cilician poet of the 3rd century B.C., author of a poem on natural phenomena, from which these words are taken.

to the speech, which otherwise stands in a Jewish tradition going back to Old Testament times.[9]

Christianity in the Roman Empire

In these defences against Judaism and pagan Hellenism there is not lacking a polemical element; the attack is pressed home into the other camp. It is different with the defence against Roman law; Luke, like most of the New Testament writers, cultivates the good-will of Roman law and of administrative authority in general throughout the Empire.

But what of the undeniable fact that Jesus had been convicted and executed on a charge of sedition against Caesar? Luke's answer to this is one which he shares with his fellow-evangelists, although he develops it in his own way. The condemnation of Jesus was a miscarriage of justice: Pontius Pilate did indeed pass the death-sentence on him, but reluctantly and against his better judgment, yielding to the pressure of the chief priests. When Jesus' prosecutors charged him with subverting the Jewish nation, forbidding them to pay tribute to Caesar[10] and claiming a messianic kingship for himself, Pilate found no substance in the charges. When he tried to remit the case to Herod Antipas, tetrarch of Galilee,[11] who was then resident in Jerusalem, Herod equally found him guilty of no capital offence. Pilate would have had him scourged and discharged, but at last gave in to the chief priests' insistence and condemned him to the cross. Even then, one of the bandits crucified alongside him testified that this man had committed no act of insurgency such as he himself and his comrade had committed, and the Roman officer on duty at the place of execution acknowledged that he was certainly innocent.[12]

If in Part I Luke maintains that, despite the record, Jesus was no rebel against Rome, in Part II he defends Christianity against the charge that its progress through the Roman provinces was attended by rioting and breaches of the peace. Unseemly outbreaks of this

[9] Cf. Psalm 50: 7–13; Isa. 44: 9–20; 66: 1f.
[10] Luke 23: 2. This charge involved a radical perversion of Jesus' response on this subject in Luke 20: 25 (Mark 12: 17).
[11] See p. 20.
[12] See p. 21 for Mark's treatment of the centurion's words. Luke takes them as an admission of Jesus' guiltlessness, so as to serve his own apologetic purpose.

character had indeed occurred, but these were stirred up by Jewish opponents of the gospel or by Gentile property interests which (as at Philippi and Ephesus) felt themselves menaced by its advance. Civic and provincial authorities repeatedly exonerated the Christian missionaries from complicity in the kind of messianic agitation which was rife among the Jewish communities throughout the Empire. Gallio, proconsul of Achaia, found Paul and his associates innocent of any "wrongdoing or vicious crime" (Acts 18: 14), and his judgment, negative as it was in form, constituted in effect a precedent which afforded them the protection of Roman law for several years to come.[13] Encouraged by his favourite experience of Roman law, Paul confidently availed himself of his right as a Roman citizen and appealed to Caesar when he could not be sure of receiving an unbiassed trial from the procurator of Judaea (Acts 25: 11); and Luke brings his history to an end with the picture of Paul under house-arrest in Rome, waiting for his appeal to be heard, and meanwhile preaching the gospel at the heart of the Empire to all who came to see him, "quite openly and unhindered" (Acts 28: 31), without any attempt at interference on the part of the imperial officers. So far was Christianity from being a threat to the Roman state!

The Gentile Mission

Luke's theological emphasis is nowhere more clearly expressed than in Paul's last recorded words near the end of his history: "Let it be known to you then that this salvation of God has been sent to the Gentiles; they will listen" (Acts 28: 28). The same emphasis appears at the beginning of his narrative: Simeon of Jerusalem, holding the infant Jesus in his arms, thanks God because, as he says (Luke 2: 30–32):

> mine eyes have seen thy salvation
> which thou hast prepared in the presence of all peoples,
> a light for revelation to the Gentiles,
> and for glory to thy people Israel.

The worldwide salvation of God, embodied in Jesus and proclaimed in the gospel, is Luke's dominant concern. The

[13] In fact, until Nero's attack on the Christians of Rome from A.D. 64 onwards (see p. 19).

announcement of "a light for revelation to the Gentiles", echoing the language of the Servant's commission in Isa. 49: 6, is realized in the Gentile mission of Part II; indeed, Paul and Barnabas in Acts 13: 47 claim that very language as their own commission for preaching to the Gentiles: "For so the Lord has commanded us, saying,

'I have set you to be a light for the Gentiles,
that you may bring salvation to the uttermost parts of the earth'."

In the same vein, when Luke (like the other evangelists) quotes Isa. 40: 3 ("The voice of one crying. . .") at the outset of his account of John the Baptist's ministry, he lets the quotation run on for longer than it does in the other Gospels, until it concludes on the triumphant note: "and all flesh shall see the salvation of God" (Luke 3: 4–6).

The programme of the saving mission of Jesus is clearly set out in the report of his address in the Nazareth synagogue, which Luke takes out of its chronological sequence and places in the forefront of his record of the Galilaean ministry (Luke 4: 16–30). On that sabbath day Jesus read and expounded the second lesson, the opening clauses of Isa. 61:

The Spirit of the Lord is upon me,
because he has anointed me to preach good news to the poor.
He has sent me to proclaim release to the captives
and recovering of sight to the blind,
to set at liberty those who are oppressed,
to proclaim the acceptable year of the Lord.

(It is noteworthy that the words which in Isa. 61: 2 stand in synonymous parallelism with "the acceptable year of the Lord" – "and the day of vengeance of our God" – are omitted. Apposite as they would have been to John the Baptist's preaching, they found no place in the early Galilaean message of Jesus.)

Jesus' exposition of the text begins with the announcement, "Today this scripture has been fulfilled in your hearing." A message of liberation was the appropriate message for "the acceptable year of the Lord" – a phrase primarily denoting the recurring year of release. This may not have been a jubilee year according to the calendar, when the trumpet was sounded to "proclaim liberty throughout the land to all its inhabitants" (Lev. 25: 10), but the authentic jubilee proclamation was sounded. The preaching of "good news to the poor" is taken to mean the assurance of God's grace to the underprivileged in general: the Old Testament illustrations adduced to drive the lesson home tell how, in the days of Elijah and Elisha, non-Israelites like the widow of Zarephath[14] and Naaman the Syrian[15] were singled out for special blessing, when Israelites in equal need were passed over. Luke, who himself was probably a Gentile, records this exposition of the prophetic text with particular satisfaction, in view of his later account of the Gentile mission; it is hardly surprising, however, that the Nazareth congregation listened to it with less than pleasure. People who have taken their privileges for granted find it disagreeable to be suddenly bereft of them.

Good News to the Poor

The emphasis on "good news to the poor" reappears in Jesus' message to John the Baptist. As John in prison heard reports of the Galilaean ministry, he may well have wondered what this ministry had in common with the activity he had forecast for the Coming One, whose "winnowing fork is in his hand, to clear his threshing floor, and to gather the wheat into his granary, but the chaff he will burn with unquenchable fire" (Luke 3: 17). This bore little resemblance to "the wrath to come", the hewing down and burning of fruitless trees of which he had warned his hearers (Luke 3: 7–9). Hence the question which, at his bidding, his two disciples put to Jesus: "Are you the Coming One, or shall we look for someone else?" (Luke 7: 19f).[16] Jesus kept them with him while he performed many of his acts of healing, and sent them back to tell John what they had seen and heard: "the blind receive their sight, the lame walk, lepers are cleansed, and the deaf hear, the dead are raised up, the poor have good news preached to them" (Luke 7: 22). This message was calculated to reassure John that in the current ministry

[14] Cf. I Kings 17: 8ff.
[15] Cf. II Kings 5: 1ff.
[16] Cf. the parallel account in Matt. 11: 3.

of Jesus the ancient prophecies of the new age were being fulfilled,[17] and pre-eminently so in the preaching of good news to the poor.

In Part I of Luke's history the underprivileged are, with one exception, not Gentiles. The exception is the centurion of Capernaum whose servant was cured, and of whom Jesus said: "not even in Israel have I found such faith" (Luke 7: 9).[18] It is remarkable that Luke does not reproduce Mark's incident of the healing of the Syrophoenician girl;[19] indeed, he omits the whole section of Mark in which this incident occurs (Mark 6: 45–8: 26) – a section which some theologians have interpreted as an adumbration of the Gentile mission. Perhaps he omitted this section because he was reserving the Gentile mission for Part II. (Another episode in this section is Jesus' pronouncement in Mark 7: 18f which in effect "declared all foods clean"; this is a subject to which Luke gives prominent treatment in the Cornelius narrative of Acts 10.)

The underprivileged who in the Gospel of Luke receive special consideration and show special appreciation are (in addition to the literal poor) women, Samaritans, tax-collectors and sinners. The description of Jesus as "a friend of tax-collectors and sinners" belongs to the material common to Matthew and Luke (Matt. 11: 19; Luke 7: 34),[20] but it is Luke who distinctively elaborates this theme, in narrative and parable alike. The disapproving comment, "This man receives sinners and eats with them" (Luke 15: 2), forms the introduction to the three parables of the lost sheep, the lost coin and the lost son, which emphasize that in heaven, as on earth, the recovery of something or someone that has been lost is celebrated with much more excitement than the continued possession of what has never gone amissing.

The Age of Salvation

Over the age inaugurated by the coming of Christ Luke would not have hesitated to write, in the words with which Paul interprets the prophetic language of Isa. 49: 8, "Behold, now is the acceptable

[17] In addition to Isa. 61: 1f, cf. Isa. 35: 5f.
[18] Cf. the parallel account in Matt. 8: 10.
[19] Mark 7: 24–30 (cf. Matt. 15: 21–28).
[20] For a Markan counterpart cf. the call of Levi and its sequel in Mark 2: 13–17.

time; behold, now is the day of salvation" (II Cor. 6: 2). This new age has dawned in fulfilment of the purpose of God declared in ages past. Luke is fond of using in this connexion verbs or verbal nouns compounded with the Greek prefix *pro*, meaning "before". Jesus was delivered up to his enemies "according to the definite plan and *foreknowledge* of God" (Acts 2: 23); his enemies did whatever the hand and plan of God "had *foreordained* to take place" (Acts 4: 28); through his prophets God "*foretold*. . . that his Christ should suffer" (Acts 3: 18; cf. 7: 52); David "*foresaw* and spoke of the resurrection of Christ" (Acts 2: 31), and so on. The same idea is expressed by the repeated emphasis on the divine necessity of the passion of Christ: "Was it not necessary that the Christ should suffer these things and enter into his glory?" (Luke 24: 26; cf. 24: 46; Acts 3: 18; 17: 3; 26: 23). Paul's synagogue address at Pisidian Antioch (Acts 13: 16–41), which fills a programmatic rôle in the second half of Acts similar to that of Jesus' Nazareth address in Luke's Gospel, expounds this theme of fulfilment in detail, showing how the history of Israel, especially the delivering act of God at the Exodus and the setting of David on his throne, with the promises made regarding his dynasty,[21] led on to the coming of Jesus, in whose ministry, death and resurrection the pattern of deliverance reached its consummation and the promises were confirmed. The story of Jesus is the message of salvation.

The age of salvation is treated by Luke in two stages, corresponding to the two parts of his history: in the former phase Jesus is himself active on earth in bodily form; in the latter he is enthroned in the presence of God, but his power (his "name", as Luke likes to put it) is active on earth by the agency of the Holy Spirit, who came down on the day of Pentecost in accordance with Jesus' promise to his disciples. Part II of Luke's work has sometimes been called, not inappropriately, "The Acts of the Holy Spirit".[22]

When John the Baptist pointed forward to the advent of the one who was mightier than himself, he said, "I baptize you with water; but he. . .will baptize you with the Holy Spirit and with fire"

[21] Cf. Acts 2: 30f, where the dynastic promise to David (formulated, e.g., in II Sam. 7: 12ff; Psalm 132: 11ff) is interpreted as fulfilled in the resurrection of Christ.

[22] As in the title of A. T. Pierson, *The Acts of the Holy Spirit* (London, 1913); cf. J. H. E. Hull, *The Holy Spirit in the Acts of the Apostles* (London, 1967).

(Luke 3: 16). The baptism with fire (an outpouring of judgment, according to Luke 3: 17) is not stressed when the fulfilment of John's prediction is recorded; although there may be an allusion to it in the "tongues as of fire" which rested on the disciples at Pentecost. Before his ascension the risen Christ says to his disciples, "John baptized with water, but before many days you shall be baptized with the Holy Spirit" (Acts 1: 5). For Luke, then, the event of Pentecost is the historic baptism or outpouring of the Spirit. It fulfils not only John's prediction but also the promise of God through an Old Testament prophet that "in the last days" he would pour out his Spirit "upon all flesh" (Acts 2: 17, quoting Joel 2: 28). What began that day in Jerusalem was to spread out into the whole world. The presence of the Spirit is the sign of the "last days", but the "last days" must be sufficiently extensive for the universal dissemination of the gospel.[23] It is indeed because of the presence of the Spirit that the gospel spreads so effectively as it does. The kingdom of God, present in the ministry of Jesus (cf. Luke 11: 20), is still being preached by Paul in Rome at the end of Luke's narrative (Acts 28: 31). Jesus himself began his ministry "full of the Spirit" (Luke 4: 1, 14); but that special fulness of the Spirit which his followers received from Pentecost onwards was the means by which the kingdom of God was launched with power. The power from on high has been bestowed; "now let it work!"

[23] Cf. Mark 13: 10, "the gospel must first be preached to all nations".

Six

Jesus Christ the Teacher

The Message of the Gospel of Matthew

A BODY WHICH DEPENDS SO LARGELY AS THE EARLY CHRISTIAN church did on a succession of teachers will find it useful to have manuals of instruction. Such manuals, indeed, are not indispensable; the Jewish rabbis for several generations relied chiefly on oral instruction and retentive memories; the ideal disciple was compared by one rabbi to "a well-cemented cistern which does not lose a drop."[1] Jesus, whom his contemporaries recognized as a rabbi, committed none of his teaching to writing; whether he taught the crowds publicly or his disciples privately, he taught by word of mouth. It has been suggested that some of his hearers made written notes of what he said; this possibility cannot be excluded, but there is no positive evidence to support it.

The Christian church, however, was a reading and writing community from an early stage of its existence, and as the faith spread into the Gentile world, the need for teachers and manuals of instruction must have been increasingly felt and supplied. The main substance of these manuals would have been the teaching of Jesus. From the later part of the first century comes the classic manual of Christian instruction which we call the Gospel of Matthew. The final scene of this Gospel is the appearance of the risen Christ to his apostles on a Galilaean mountain, where he gives them his parting commission: "Go . . . and make disciples of all nations . . . teaching them to observe all that I have commanded you" (Matt. 28: 19f).

---

[1] So Rabbi Yohanan ben Zakkai described his disciple Eliezer ben Hyrcanus (*Pirqe Aboth* ii. 11).

This teaching commission was to be fulfilled not only by the apostles in person but by their disciples in turn; this is indicated by the words of assurance immediately following which are not confined to the apostolic generation: "and lo, I am with you always, to the close of the age" (Matt. 28: 20).

Although no earlier manual of Christian instruction has been preserved to us, there is internal evidence in the Gospel of Matthew itself that there were earlier and shorter works of this kind, one or two of which were probably incorporated by this evangelist in his fuller work. One of these appears to have been a compilation of sayings of Jesus, set in a skeleton framework of narrative, on which Luke also drew for his Gospel. It contained the material common to Matthew and Luke which is not paralleled in Mark, and it is commonly denoted by the letter Q.[1] It may have proved useful, in its Greek version or versions, to the Gentile mission based on Antioch. Some students have discerned in this Gospel, also, evidence of a parallel compilation of sayings more closely linked with the Jewish Christianity of Jerusalem and the surrounding territory, which might have been serviceable in debates with Pharisees; this has been labelled M. Whatever the truth may be about such earlier compilations, our evangelist has gathered the sayings of Jesus into five bodies of discourse-material, each dealing with a well-defined range of subject-matter, and set them in a narrative framework consisting largely of an abridgement of Mark's Gospel, with the order of the earlier part rearranged so as to suit the associated discourses.[2] To the whole is prefaced a prologue, the infancy narrative of the first two chapters, while an epilogue relates two resurrection appearances, one in Jerusalem and one in Galilee (Matt. 28: 9–20).

[1] It has frequently been suggested that this was the work referred to by Papias (bishop of Hierapolis in Phrygia *c.* A.D. 130): "Matthew compiled the oracles in the Hebrew speech, and everyone translated them as best as he could" (quoted by Eusebius, *Hist. Eccl.* iii. 39. 16).

[2] Thus, if the Sermon on the Mount (Matt. 5–7) presents the authority of Jesus in word, the incidents of chapters 8 and 9 present his authority in deed. Particularly noteworthy is the collocation of the stilling of the tempest (8: 23–27), which reveals him as Lord of winds and waves, curbing the unruly forces of chaos as the Creator did in the Old Testament (e.g. Psalm 89: 9), with the healing of the Gadarene demoniac (8: 28–34), which reveals him as Lord over spiritual powers, mastering a tempest of a more intractable nature.

The King of Israel

Matthew's Gospel emphasizes Jesus' teaching ministry: it is distinctively the Gospel of Jesus Christ the Teacher.

But this is interwoven with another theme: Jesus Christ the King. This theme is present in some degree in all the Gospels: the four evangelists agree in telling how the inscription above Jesus' head on the cross proclaimed him to be "The King of the Jews", and John brings out the significance of his kingship in his report of Jesus' answers to Pilate's interrogation (John 18: 33–38).[4] But Matthew makes a special point of emphasizing at the outset of his work that Jesus is the legal heir to David's throne. His descent is traced from Abraham through David and the members of David's dynasty who occupied the throne in succession after him, from Solomon to Jeconiah (Jehoiachin), who was carried into exile by the Babylonians. Luke also has a genealogical list which traces Jesus' lineage back through David to Adam (Luke 3: 23–38), but in Luke's list the generations after David are represented not by the kings who sat on his throne but by commoners – by the descendants of Nathan, a son of David for whom no claim to royal estate was made. Between David and Joseph, Jesus' adoptive father, the two lists coincide briefly only in Shealtiel and his son Prince Zerubbabel,[5] the latter of whom served as governor of Judaea for a few years after the return from the Babylonian exile. Luke is concerned to emphasize Jesus' solidarity with the human race; Matthew aims at establishing his title to the throne of David, and some links in his claim may denote the legal succession rather than the literal father-and-son relationship.

When, therefore, Matthew goes on to tell how the magi from the east came to Judaea seeking the new-born King of the Jews, whose star they had seen at its rising (Matt. 2: 1f), his readers are already aware of the King's identity and title. Nor are they surprised to learn how the news of his birth causes agitation in Jerusalem, where another King of the Jews has already been reigning for many years by grace of the Romans. Moreover, as a true king is the representative

---

[4] See p. 110. Early in John's narrative Nathanael hails Jesus as "the King of Israel" (John 1: 49); the same title is given him later by the pilgrim crowds at his entry into Jerusalem (John 12: 13).

[5] Matt. 1: 12f; Luke 3: 27.

and embodiment of his people, Jesus is presented as the authentic Israel. Matthew selects oracles relating to various phases of Israel's history and weaves them into his nativity narrative as *testimonia* of Jesus' identity. As Israel in its infancy went down into Egypt, for example, and was brought back by divine power, so the infant Jesus goes down into Egypt and is brought back to the land of Israel, "to fulfil what the Lord had spoken by the prophet, 'Out of Egypt have I called my son'" (Matt. 2: 15, quoting Hosea 11: 1). *Testimonia* introduced by a fulfilment formula are a recurrent feature of Matthew's Gospel, but it is only in the nativity narrative that they have this special significance.

While this introductory section of the Gospel portrays Jesus as King of the Jews, it contains indications that his coming is not for Israel only. The church has not been mistaken in interpreting the visit of the magi to pay homage to the infant King as his epiphany to the Gentiles, in fulfilment of the scripture, "nations shall come to your light, and kings to the brightness of your rising" (Isa. 60: 3). And the genealogy itself, while it confirms Jesus' royal status, hints at the Gentiles' interest in him by including the names of four women who were his ancestresses – not the matriarchs of Israel but Tamar the Canaanite, Rahab of Jericho, Ruth the Moabite, and Bathsheba, former wife of Uriah the Hittite.

But when the nativity narrative comes to an end and the story of the ministry is taken up, the theme of kingship recedes into the background. Now and again we catch a hint of it, as when Mark's statement that, on one occasion when Jesus crossed the lake of Galilee with his disciples, "they took him with them, just as he was, in the boat" (Mark 4: 36), appears in Matthew's account as "when he got into the boat, his disciples followed him" (Matt. 8: 23). This might of course, be the proper procedure for a teacher with his disciples, but it might be regarded here as the proper procedure for a king with his subjects. The note of kingship is explicit in Matthew's description of Jesus' entry into Jerusalem, with its quotation of the *testimonium* "Behold, your king" from Zech. 9: 9[6] and its rendering

* The Zechariah oracle is quoted also in John's narrative (John 12: 15). Luke reports the crowds as shouting, "Blessed is the King who comes in the name of the Lord!" (Luke 19: 38).

of the multitude's acclamation in the form, "Hosanna to the Son of David!" (Matt. 21: 5, 9).[7]

At the end of the Gospel the two rôles – of king and of teacher – are combined, for when the risen Christ commissions the apostles to "make disciples of all nations", he does so as the one invested with universal sovereignty: "All authority in heaven and on earth has been given to me. Go therefore . . ." (Matt. 28: 18f).

The Kingdom of Heaven

It is, however, pre-eminently as the Teacher that Matthew presents the one of whom he writes. The over-all subject of the teaching is the kingdom of God or, as Matthew prefers to call it, "the kingdom of heaven". His perspective is concentrated largely on the coming consummation of this kingdom; it is perhaps not an accident that in the saying of Jesus which refers most explicitly to the kingdom as already realized in the events of the ministry he retains, with Luke, the phrase "kingdom of God": "if it is by the Spirit of God that I cast out demons, then the kingdom of God has come upon you" (Matt. 12: 28; cf. Luke 11: 20).[8] In this Gospel generally, the kingdom of heaven, whose imminence is proclaimed by Jesus during his ministry (Matt. 4: 17) – and indeed by John before him (Matt. 3: 2) – is to be established fully when he comes in glory as the Son of Man (Matt. 16: 27f). But here and now the hidden powers or "secrets of the kingdom of heaven" (Matt. 13: 11) are at work and accessible by faith to the disciples of Jesus, in whose lives the ethical and social principles of the kingdom manifest themselves, so that they are the true "sons of the kingdom" (Matt. 13: 38).

Of the five bodies of discourse-material into which Matthew has gathered Jesus' teaching about the kingdom, the first, commonly called the Sermon on the Mount (Matt. 5: 1–7: 27), deals with what may be called the law of the kingdom; the second (10: 5–42) with the proclamation of the kingdom; the third (13: 1–52), comprising seven parables, with the extension of the kingdom; the fourth (18:

---

[7] "Hosanna to the Son of David" means more or less "God save the King". In none of the Gospels does Jesus claim to be Son of David, but he does not repudiate the title when it is given to him, as e.g. by Bartimaeus (Mark 10: 47f).
[8] Other occurrences of "the kingdom of God" in this Gospel are Matt. 19: 24; 21: 31, 43.

1–35) with the fellowship of the kingdom; the fifth (23: 1–25: 46), culminating in three parables, with the consummation of the kingdom. Each of the five is concluded by some such words as "And when Jesus had finished these sayings . . ." (Matt. 7: 28; cf. 11: 1; 13: 53; 19: 1; 26: 1). Some further teaching occurs outside the limits of these discourses, such as the parables of the labourers in the vineyard (Matt. 20: 1–16)[9] and of the wedding feast (22: 1–14).

The Sermon on the Mount

The "mountain" from which the first body of teaching is delivered (Matt. 5: 1) has not only geographical significance (although it can be located with considerable confidence): in this Gospel especially the mountain is the place of revelation (we may compare the mountain of transfiguration in Matt. 17: 1 and the mountain where the risen Christ appeared to the eleven in 28: 16). If the subject-matter of the Sermon on the Mount is called the "law" of the kingdom, it is no law that can be enforced by temporal sanctions, like the earlier law promulgated from Mount Sinai. The qualities singled out for approbation in the beatitudes of Matt. 5: 3–10 cannot be enacted by statute; they are identical with the "fruit of the Spirit" described by Paul in Gal. 5: 22f, and the only "law" which can ensure their cultivation is the "law of the Spirit of life in Christ Jesus" (Rom. 8: 2). Overt words and actions can be regulated by ordinary law-codes, but not the angry thought or the concupiscent glance which precedes and gives rise to them (Matt. 5: 21–30). Religious practices which can be seen and heard are attended by subtle temptations: the real man is the man as he is when he is alone in the presence of God (6: 1–18). Worldly wealth, which passes away, is not the chief end of man; God's kingdom and righteousness must be sought above all else, and other interests will then take their appropriate place (6: 33).

The teaching of the kingdom is well summed up in the successive clauses of the Lord's Prayer (Matt. 6: 9–13), which inculcates an attitude of childlike trust in the heavenly Father for material and spiritual provision, a desire to see his will done (for in the doing of his will his kingdom comes and his name is sanctified), a spirit of

* See p. 30.

67

forgiveness towards others and an awareness of the constant need of divine guidance and protection.[10]

This teaching, Jesus assures his hearers, provides the firm foundation for life; to ignore it is to invite catastrophe (7: 24–27). Yet he impressed on them that to follow it was no light undertaking: it controverted the accepted canons not only of self-interest and power politics but of legal rectitude and prudential morality. The ethical standard which, partly by precept but much more by example, he laid down for his followers "lies not in a code, nor in a social order. It lies in a life where love to God and man is the spring of every thought and word and action: and for Christians the sum of all morality is to have the same mind which was also in Christ Jesus."[11]

The Mission of the Twelve

The second discourse finds its starting point in the commission given by Jesus to the twelve when he sent them out two by two to proclaim in word and action the approach of the kingdom; this mission of theirs was an extension of his own Galilaean ministry (Matt. 10: 5–15). But as the discourse proceeds, it embraces within its perspective a later situation, when they would be exposed to prosecution and punishment before synagogue authorities and pagan courts, as they were not during their brief preaching and healing tour in Galilee. This part of the discourse (10: 16–23) may envisage the circumstances of their ministry to Israel in the generation stretching from Jesus' resurrection to the outbreak of the war against Rome in A.D. 66 (cf. Gal. 2: 7–9). The main lesson is summed up in verses 24 and 25, where the twelve are warned not to expect better treatment than that meted out to their Master: "A disciple is not above his teacher, nor a servant above his master; it is enough for the disciple to be like his teacher, and the servant like his master."

Parables of the Kingdom

In the third discourse the extension of the kingdom is illustrated by the parables of the seed sown in four kinds of soil (13: 3–23), of the

[10] See also p. 71 with n. 14. The Lord's Prayer is given in a shorter and probably more primitive form in Luke 11: 2–4.

[11] T. W. Manson, *The Teaching of Jesus* (Cambridge, 1935), p. 312.

tares among the wheat (13: 24–30, 36–43), of the mustard seed (13: 31f), the leaven (13: 33), the hidden treasure (13: 44), the pearl of great price (13: 45f) and the dragnet (13: 47–50). These parables stress the kingdom's inconspicuous beginnings and its glorious manifestation on the day when the final separation between good and evil is made. That final separation sets the seal on a separation which is taking place here and now, as the "sons of the kingdom" and the "sons of the evil one" reveal themselves by their opposite reactions to the person and proclamation of Jesus.

The discourse of chapter 13, in fact, marks the turning-point of this Gospel. Jesus has been repudiated by the religious leaders; his works of mercy and power have been put down to demonic possession. In reply, he affirms that for those who deliberately ascribe to Beelzebul the work of the Spirit of God there is no further hope; to them the plainest teaching about the kingdom is henceforth meaningless because, like those to whom Isaiah preached in his day, they have rendered themselves incapable of seeing, hearing or understanding (13: 13–15). But to unprejudiced hearers his message comes home, like good seed falling into good soil, and they see and hear things which prophets and righteous men longed in vain to see and hear. This was true not only in the situation of the ministry: the Christian community in which this Gospel appeared had similarly experienced the unresponsiveness of contemporary rabbinic Judaism, but the sons of the kingdom – individual Jews as well as Gentiles – continued to identify themselves as such by accepting the challenge of Jesus, communicated through his followers of a later generation. And "today, too, even as at the time of Matthew, the parables of Jesus can be seen to be an instrument of God for raising up 'sons of the Kingdom': people who, as Matthew would put it, discover the joy of knowing and doing the will of God."[12]

The Fellowship of the Kingdom

The fourth discourse begins with emphasis on the spirit of child-like simplicity which is the indispensable condition for entering the kingdom of heaven, not to speak of attaining a position of greatness

[12] J. D. Kingsbury, *The Parables of Jesus in Matthew 13* (London, 1969), p. 137.

in it (18: 1–4). Some words follow on the paramount importance of showing special consideration to children and those who share the simplicity of children: to lead such "little ones" astray is to sentence one's own soul to death (18: 5–14). The mutual responsibilities of "sons of the kingdom" are then taken up – the responsibility, for example, of restoring a brother who errs from the right path (18: 15–20) and above all, the duty of unlimited forgiveness (18: 21f), illustrated by the parable of the unforgiving servant (18: 23–35). The hard saying at the end of the parable – "So also my heavenly Father will do to every one of you, if you do not forgive your brother from your heart" – is not to be glossed over or explained away; if it cannot be accommodated easily within our theological system, it is the system that should be modified to make room for it in its natural sense.

One of the two occurrences of the word "church" in the Gospels is found in this discourse (18: 17); the other also comes in this Gospel, in Jesus' words to Peter, "on this rock I will build my church" (16: 18). There the church extending throughout space and time is probably meant, but here the context points to a particular group of Jesus' disciples, two or three gathered together in his name and invested by him with disciplinary authority and the right of prevailing access to God in prayer.

The Close of the Age

The final discourse, which is set in Jerusalem, is preceded by a denunciation of those "scribes and Pharisees" whose practice fell too far short of their preaching (Matt. 23: 1–36). We should remember that of seven types of Pharisee distinguished in rabbinic tradition only one, he who is a Pharisee for love of God, receives unqualified commendation;[18] we should remember, too, that the credibility gap between religious profession and performance which calls forth this denunciation is not unknown among those who claim to be Jesus' followers, and is all the more reprehensible on that account.

Unwelcome in the Jerusalem temple as in the synagogues of Galilee, Jesus abandons the sacred buildings with the words, "you will

---

[18] Palestinian Talmud, *Berakoth* ix. 7.

not see me again, until you say, 'Blessed is he who comes in the name of the Lord'" (23: 39), and predicts their impending destruction (24: 1f). This prediction leads to the disciples' request for further details (23: 3) – a request framed in Matthew's account in such a way as to distinguish clearly between the fall of the temple (which had perhaps taken place recently when this Gospel was published) and "the close of the age" (which, of course, lay in the future). Matthew's version of Jesus' answer to the twofold question (24: 4–44) keeps in step with the Olivet discourse of Mark 13: 5–37, and ends with a solemn and repeated warning to be ready for the unknown and unexpected day and hour when the Son of Man comes. The warning is reinforced by the short parable of the faithful and unfaithful servant (24: 45–51) and by the three great parables of the ten virgins (25: 1–13), the talents (25: 14–30) and the sheep and the goats (25: 31–46). The admonition at the end of the parable of the ten virgins, "Watch therefore, for you know neither the day nor the hour" (25: 13), has been amplified in the traditional text by the added clause "when the Son of man comes". The added clause may be exegetically sound, but the unaugmented text bids us be ready for any hour of testing that may come unannounced. Be ready (so the lesson runs) to resist the temptation (whatever form it may take), to meet the crisis, to grasp the opportunity. Yesterday's oil will not keep our lamps alight today; past experience is not in itself sufficient for present or future need. Jesus had taught his disciples to pray that they might not fail in the great test of faith (Matt. 6: 13) and just before his arrest he urged them afresh to "keep awake and pray not to fail in the test" (26– 41).[14] The test came and found them unprepared, but their sorry failure was redressed when their exalted Lord appeared to them in Galilee and in the exercise of his unrestricted authority gave them a wider and more enduring commission than before. Henceforth he would be with them in even greater power than when he was visibly at their head, and in his abiding presence they had the assurance that their worldwide ministry would accomplish his purpose.

[14] This, rather than the NEB "do not bring us to the test" (also in Luke 11: 4) and "pray that you may be spared the test" (from Mark 14: 38), is the probable sense of these passages. The test could not be avoided; what was required was faith sufficiently strong to stand firm in it.

The Message of the New Testament

The Well-Trained Scribe

Matthew provided the Christians for whom he wrote with a volume of instruction in the propagation and defence of the message with which they had been entrusted, and so effective was the provision he made, for them and for all their successors, that his work quickly attained, and has ever since retained, pride of place at the head of the church's fourfold Gospel. In him was realized in a distinguished degree his Master's picture of the ideal "scribe who has been trained for the kingdom of heaven" and "brings out of his treasure what is new and what is old" (Matt. 13: 52).

Seven

Unchanging and Onward-Moving

The Message of Hebrews

NOT ALL FOLLOWERS OF JESUS IN THE FIRST CENTURY WERE HAPPY to think of Christianity as a faith for the world. The extension of the Gentile mission called for outward-looking Christians, whereas many religious people are by temperament and preference inward-looking. In a closed fellowship they can worship God in established and congenial forms, but the extension of its boundaries and the large-scale incorporation of people with different backgrounds from their own must bring unwelcome changes. The spirit of adventure makes no appeal to them – least of all adventure in the realm of religion.

The Setting of the Letter to the Hebrews

It was in all probability to a conservative community of this kind that the anonymous document traditionally called the Letter to the Hebrews was addressed. The members of this community – a group of Jewish Christians, it appears, possibly resident in Rome – had never heard or seen Jesus in person, but had learned of him from others. Since their conversion these Christians had been exposed to quite severe persecution which they survived nobly. Although not called upon to suffer death for their faith,[1] they had had to endure *public abuse, imprisonment and looting of their property,* and through it all had given practical evidence of their faith by serving their fellow-Christians and especially by caring for those who suffered most during the time of affliction.[2]

[1] Heb. 12: 4.
[2] Heb. 10: 32–34.

73

However, by the time this letter was written, their Christian development had been arrested. Instead of pressing ahead, they were inclined to come to a halt in their spiritual progress, if not indeed to slip back. Probably they were reluctant to sever their last ties with their ancestral Jewish faith, which, after all, had certain advantages in the first century A.D. For one thing it enjoyed the protection of Roman law as a recognized and permitted religion. To abandon it completely would mean irretrievable commitment to the Christian way which enjoyed no such legal protection. So they were reluctant to burn their boats completely and commit themselves irrevocably to the new order introduced by Christ.

The writer of the letter, who had known them for some considerable time, and felt a pastoral concern for their well-being, was unable to visit them immediately, so he sent them this written homily – based, according to some scholars, on the synagogue lessons for the season of Pentecost. He warns them repeatedly against drawing back, for this might result in their falling away from their Christian profession altogether. He encourages them with the assurance that they have everything to gain if they press on, but everything to lose if they fall back. Perhaps they formed a household church within the wider fellowship of a city church and were tending to neglect the bonds of fellowship that bound them to Christians outside their own inner circle. That is why he exhorts them not to forsake their assembling together as some people were disposed to do, but to meet together and to encourage one another all the more as they saw the decisive day approaching (Heb. 10: 25).

How are such people to be helped – people who look back longingly to their ancestral faith which they learn has been superseded by something better and higher? How can they best be encouraged to press on? In this letter the writer sets himself to establish the finality of the gospel by contrast with everything that went before, more particularly with the levitical ritual of the Old Testament. By establishing the finality of Christ both in his person and in his work, he establishes the finality of the gospel as the way of perfection, the new order in which men and women enjoy uninterrupted access to God through Christ.

He demonstrates that Christ is greater than all the servants and spokesmen of God who have gone before: not only human servants and spokesmen, including Moses, but angels also. For Jesus is the Son of God, his agent in creating and maintaining the universe,[3] yet the One who became Son of Man and submitted to humiliation and death.[4] Now he is exalted far above all heavens, enthroned at God's right hand, living for ever before God as his people's representative. The special aspect of Christ's person and ministry emphasized here is his high priesthood, this letter being the only New Testament document which expressly refers to Jesus as priest, though others *imply* his priesthood.

The Priest-King

One source of our author's understanding of Christ as high priest is Psalm 110. Here in the oracle of verse 1, "Sit at my right hand till I make your enemies your footstool," and again in that of verse 4, "You are a priest for ever after the order of Melchizedek," the Messiah of Israel, the prince of the house of David, is acclaimed as both king and high priest, the perfect priest-king. But the mere quoting of an Old Testament text would have had little point if there had not been in actual fact a recognizable priestly quality about the character and work of Christ. So the high priesthood of Christ is established also on the historical facts of the character and achievement of Jesus. Stress is laid repeatedly upon his personal qualifications to be his people's effective high priest. Not only was he "holy, blameless, unstained" (Heb. 7: 26) but, having been in all points tempted like his people, he can sympathize with them and supply the help they need in the hour of trial.

This presentation of Jesus agrees completely with the testimony of the evangelists. At the last supper, when predicting Peter's fall and denial, our Lord said to him, "I have prayed for you that your faith may not fail; and when you have turned again strengthen your brethren" (Luke 22: 32). If it be asked what particular form our Lord's intercession on his people's behalf is taking at the present time, perhaps the answer is that in the presence of God, he is performing for all of them the same kind of intercessory service as he performed when on earth he prayed that Peter's faith should not fail, but

[3] Heb. 1: 1–4.
[4] Heb. 2: 5ff.

75

performing it now on the basis of his perfect self-offering, the most prevalent intercession of all.

Again in John 17 we have his prayer of consecration as he offers up his life to God on his people's behalf, and his prayer of intercession for them that they may fulfil their witness in the world as he fulfilled his. It is not surprising that for centuries this prayer has been called his high-priestly prayer.

In addition, we have his assurance to the disciples: "Everyone who acknowledges me before men, the Son of man also will acknowledge before the angels of God" (Luke 12: 8). Christians of New Testament times quickly understood the import of this. For example, Stephen, condemned by an earthly court, makes his confident appeal to the heavenly court where he sees the Son of Man standing on the right hand of God as his advocate (Acts 7: 56).

To the same effect, Paul, perhaps quoting a well-established confessional form of words some years before Hebrews was written, challenges anyone to bring a charge against God's elect, saying, "It is Christ Jesus who died, yes, who was raised from the dead, who is at the right hand of God, who indeed intercedes for us" (Rom. 8: 34). Then, later, John reminds his "little children" that "if any one does sin, we have an advocate with the Father, Jesus Christ the righteous, and he is the atonement[5] for our sins" (I John 2: 1f). John's use of the word "atonement" – an atonement of which God is the initiator and man is the beneficiary – implies a priestly element in the advocacy and intercession of the exalted Christ. So when the writer to the Hebrews presents Christ as high priest he is not introducing a complete innovation. Even if the terminology had not been used before, the idea was already present, firmly founded upon the work and teaching of Christ.

However, in this letter the priesthood of Christ is elaborated in quite a distinctive manner, in order to establish that in Christ and the gospel God has spoken his final and perfect word to mankind. Arguments of various kinds are adduced to show that the priesthood

---

[5] The word is rendered "propitiation" in AV and RV, "expiation" in RSV, "remedy for the defilement" in NEB (in keeping with the reference to cleansing in I John 1: 7; see p. 97). Whichever rendering be preferred, what is important is that the divine initiative be borne in mind; cf. Rom. 3: 25, where similarly it is God who provides Christ as the agent or locus of atonement, and Heb. 2: 17, where it is Christ who as high priest makes atonement for the people's sins.

of Christ is not only superior to that of Aaron's line but that it belongs to an entirely different order. It belongs to that new covenant foretold in Jer. 31: 31–34;[6] a covenant marked by better promises and a better hope than the old covenant of Sinai under which the priests of Aaron's line ministered. It is associated with a better sacrifice than any tnat went before and is discharged in a better sanctuary than that prescribed and constructed according to the book of Exodus. Priesthood and sacrifice inevitably go together. The priests of Aaron's line repeatedly offered up animal sacrifices, notably the annual sin-offering on the day of atonement, but these could not meet the real need of men and women. They could not cleanse the conscience from the stain of sin which posed a barrier to communion with God. In contrast, Christ exercises *his* high-priestly ministry on the basis of a real and *effective* sacrifice – the sacrifice of himself.

An Effective Sacrifice

The nature of this sacrifice is found to be adumbrated in the language of Psalm 40, where someone who knows the uselessness of animal sacrifices dedicates his life to God for the obedient accomplishment of his will. In this letter the language of the psalmist is interpreted as the language of Christ when he comes into the world.[7] In the body prepared for him he fulfilled the will of God, and at the end it was that consecrated body, that obedient life, that he offered up to God in death. Such a sacrifice of perfect obedience must necessarily be acceptable to God, and not only so, but it also effectually cleanses in heart and conscience those who embrace Christ as their sacrifice and high priest with God. By the will of God which Christ fulfilled in death as in life, his people have been sanctified once for all and "have confidence to enter the sanctuary by the blood of Jesus" (Heb. 10: 19). Further, thanks to the efficacy of his sacrifice in the lives of his people, the new covenant comes into being in which God undertakes to implant his law in their hearts as it was implanted in the heart of Christ, and to remember their sins no more.

---

[6] Quoted in Heb. 8: 8–12.
[7] Heb. 10: 5–7, quoting the Greek text of Psalm 40: 6–8.

How was the writer so certain of the efficacy of the sacrifice of Christ? He quotes Psalm 110 and Psalm 40, but from these he could not readily have inferred the efficacy of the sacrifice of Christ on behalf of sinners apart from the fulfilment of the words of the Psalter by the work of Christ. When he wrote the letter the efficacy of the sacrifice of Christ was already a matter of vital experience for a whole generation of believers. They knew that through the Christ who died and rose again they had been inwardly purified from the defilement of sin and emancipated from its domination. In this letter the truth is expressed in terms of sacrifice and priesthood, but the truth itself was no new thing.

He who offers up his life to God in unreserved consecration is both priest and sacrifice at once. This is true of the speaker in Psalm 40. It is even more explicitly true of the Servant of the Lord in the book of Isaiah. In Hebrews 9: 28 the willing self-offering of the Servant of the Lord to bear the sins of many is expressly interpreted of the work of Christ, the words "to bear the sins of many" being a straight quotation from Isaiah 53: 12. In Isaiah 52: 15 the Servant has been introduced as destined to "sprinkle many nations", and this sprinkling can best be understood as part of the priestly work of cleansing. Thus the Servant of the Lord is presented as a priest, making purification for men, and equally as a sacrifice, yielding himself up as an offering for their sin. In this spirit our Lord accepted death, and the redemptive and cleansing efficacy of his death in the lives of his followers has been a matter of plain experience throughout nineteen centuries. The writer of Hebrews is not airily theorizing when he speaks of priesthood and sacrifice. He is expressing basic realities of the Christian life. If we translate his emphasis into less pictorial terms than he uses, we may say that our Lord's death, and the spirit in which he accepted death, constitute an abiding force in the eternal order, powerfully acting in our defence. The crucified and exalted Jesus is the representative man, the perpetual "guardian of mankind".

Such a sacrifice as the sacrifice of Christ needs no repetition, nor is repetition possible. Its once-for-all character involves the finality of the gospel, God's final revelation of himself to mankind, because the sacrifice of Christ is perfect. The sanctuary where Christ now ministers as high priest in the presence of God is naturally superior to any other holy place, and the priesthood which is exercised there is naturally superior to any exercised in an earthly sanctuary. In the heavenly and eternal sanctuary his people inevitably enjoy more direct and permanent access to God through him than would be possible in any material shrine.

The House of God

But just how is this heavenly and eternal sanctuary envisaged? We should not think that because our author speaks of Jesus as having passed through the heavens and sat down at the right hand of God, the heavenly sanctuary is distinguished from the earthly simply in the fact that it is established in perpetuity on some higher plane. The language used is indeed pictorial but it denotes realities of the spiritual order in which men and women, inwardly purified from a sin-stained conscience, draw near to God to worship him in spirit and in truth. The sanctuary in which believers worship God through Christ is the fellowship of the new covenant. It consists in the communion of saints. The house of God over which the Son of God is Lord comprises the people of God: "we are his house if we hold fast our confidence and the glorying of our hope firm to the end" (Heb. 3: 6).

The writer thus communicates the same truth as is expressed by Paul when he speaks of Jewish and Gentile believers made one in Christ and having access in one Spirit to the Father, built together "for a dwelling-place of God in the Spirit" (Eph. 2: 18–22), or by Peter when he describes how those who have come to Christ are "built into a spiritual house, to be a holy priesthood, to offer up spiritual sacrifices acceptable to God through Jesus Christ" (I Pet. 2: 5).[8] And this same truth is seen consummated by John in the Revelation when he describes how God sets up his dwelling-place on earth and extends his covenant blessing to all peoples (Rev. 21: 3).[9]

Let us go forth

Human life has been marked by change ever since the beginning of time. Every age is an age of transition and the people to whom this

[8] See p. 92.
[9] See p. 87.

letter was written realized, rather to their discomfort, that they were living in a world from which old landmarks were disappearing. Those on whom they had once relied for instruction and help were no longer with them, though their memory and example remained. Hence the writer's exhortation: "Remember your leaders, those who spoke to you the word of God; consider the outcome of their life, and imitate their faith" (Heb. 13: 7). Great as was the help given by their former spiritual guides, those guides had died. They had passed on and were no longer available, but there was one always available – Jesus Christ, their eternal contemporary, their constant guide – Jesus Christ, the same yesterday and today and for ever. *Yesterday* he laid down his life on his people's behalf; *today* he is risen and exalted at God's right hand as their high priest and intercessor; *for ever* he lives, this same Jesus, to be to his people all they need in every conceivable situation of this life or the next.[10] Others serve their generation by the will of God and then sleep the sleep of death, but he, because he lives for ever, "holds his priesthood permanently" (Heb. 7: 24).

However, these "Hebrews" had to learn that while Christ is unchanging he is nevertheless onward-moving; always leading his people forth to new ventures in his cause; always calling them to go out not knowing where they are going, but only that it is he who is guiding them there. It was difficult for them to adjust themselves to this new situation. They were reluctant to break entirely with the familiar association of the faith of their fathers. Inside the well-loved "camp" of the old religion they felt at home, insulated from the strange and unfriendly world outside. But they had to learn that Christ was outside, claiming that strange and unfriendly world for himself. If they wanted to be his people without reservation, they must follow him outside the "camp" and throw themselves into the enterprise to which he was leading (Heb. 13: 13). "Let us go forth" might be hard advice, but "let us go forth *to him*" should not be hard advice for any Christian to accept.

Christians are what they are by virtue of certain acts of God which took place at a definite time in the past. But those acts of God, his redemptive acts in the death and resurrection of Christ, have released a force which will never allow Christians to stay put or stick

[10] Cf. Heb. 7: 25.

in the mud. The faith once for all delivered to the saints is not something we can catch and tame. It is dynamic; always leading us farther afield.

It was because of Abraham's faith in the unchanging God that he was so ready to go forth at God's bidding, not knowing where he might be led.[11] To stay, out of a mistaken sense of loyalty, at the point to which some revered teacher of the past may have brought us, to continue to follow a certain pattern of religious activity just because it was good enough for our fathers and grandfathers, these and the like are temptations which make the message of this letter permanently necessary and salutary. Every new movement of the Spirit of God tends to become stereotyped in the next generation. What we have heard with our ears, what our fathers have told us, becomes a tenacious tradition encroaching on the allegiance which ought to be accorded only to the living and active word of God.

As the Christian surveys the world of today he sees very much land to be possessed in the name of Christ; but to take possession of it calls for a generous measure of that forward-looking faith which is so earnestly urged upon the readers of this letter. They were living at a time when the old cherished order was breaking up. Attachment to the venerable traditions of the past could avail them nothing. The only thing that could avail was attachment to the unchanging and onward-moving Christ. This could carry them forward and enable them to face the new situation with confidence and power.

We too live in a changing world in which the old familiar landmarks are disappearing, and those to whom we looked as guides have gone on before and are no longer available to give us the kind of help they once did. But Jesus Christ remains the same and calls us to claim the new and unfamiliar world of today for him. It may seem much more comfortable to construct for ourselves right little, tight little encampments, to build walls inside which we feel at home, psychologically insulated from the world outside; content to see the old familiar faces, follow the old familiar ways, sing the old familiar hymns and forget what is happening outside. But these old familiar patterns of life are exposed to rapid change and dissolution, and the world outside, strange and even uncongenial as it may be to those who are growing older, is desperately in need of our unchanging

[11] Heb. 11: 8.

Christ. We too must reckon with the fact that, while we are heirs of the kingdom that cannot be shaken, we have here no lasting city[18] and Christ is still calling us forth to occupy fresh territory in his name. James Russell Lowell sums up the lesson for us, provided we remember that, for the Christian, truth is embodied in Christ:

> New occasions teach new duties;
> Time makes ancient good uncouth;
> They must upward still and onward
> Who would keep abreast of truth.

[18] Heb. 13: 14.

Eight

This is the Victory

The Message of the Revelation

A NORTH AMERICAN STUDENT, HAVING BEEN PERSUADED TO BUY A copy of *Today's English Version* (otherwise *Good News for Modern Man*), read through the New Testament for the first time. He found it most interesting, "but", he remarked to a friend, "I couldn't make much of that bit of science fiction at the end". Evidently he had been trying to relate the Revelation of John to an identifiable literary *genre*, and science fiction was the nearest he could get. Actually, John's Revelation belongs to the literary *genre* called "apocalyptic". This is an adjective derived from "apocalypse", the anglicized form of the Greek word for "revelation" (*apokalypsis*). "Apocalyptic" literature is so called because it deals with the revealing or "unveiling" of things normally inaccessible to human knowledge, such as the course of future events or the secrets of outer space. John's Revelation is more concerned with future events than with outer space; but another apocalypse which enjoyed great popularity in those days, the book of Enoch, had a good deal to say on this latter subject, for its hero describes what he saw while journeying through the seven heavens, and so it has much more claim to be classified as science fiction than John's Revelation has.

We call it John's Revelation, but it bears a more august title: it proclaims itself to be the "revelation of Jesus Christ, which God gave him to show to his servants what must soon take place". If we call it John's Revelation, that is because Jesus Christ, having received it from God, "made it known by sending his angel to his servant John, who bore witness to the word of God and to the testimony of Jesus Christ, even to all that he saw" (Rev. 1: 1f).

83

The angelic communication to John for the most part takes the form of successive visions. In one of the earliest of these visions John actually sees Jesus receiving the "revelation" from God. He is called up into heaven, where he sees God seated on the eternal throne, acclaimed by the worship of the heavenly host, and holding a sealed scroll in his right hand. This picture is in line with that found earlier (for example) in Dan. 10: 21, where the course of coming events on earth is already recorded in a heavenly "book of truth". In John's vision, however, the events recorded in the heavenly book cannot be enacted on earth, the divine purpose cannot be fulfilled, until the seals are broken and the scroll opened and read by someone who can establish his competence to do so. At last someone with the necessary competence arrives: at his approach he is announced as the victorious "Lion of the tribe of Judah, the Root of David" – that is, the Messsiah of Israel – but he makes his appearance as a Lamb newly slaughtered, and receives the scroll amidst universal jubilation. As he breaks one after another of the seals, events begin to take place on earth which lead up to the consummation of the divine purpose (Rev. 5: 1ff).

This is the central message of Revelation. The crucial event of all time is the sacrifice of Calvary; that was the decisive victory which has ensured the final triumph of God's cause and God's people over all the forces opposed to them.

The Setting of the Revelation

This message was specially timely for the readers to whom it was addressed. These were, in the first instance, members of seven churches in the province of Asia; more generally, they were Christians living in the Roman Empire in days when that power had adopted the policy of hostility to Christianity which it maintained for two and a half centuries. Some of them were exposed to direct persecution and might have been tempted to conclude that there was no point in holding out against the might of Rome, which was bound to win sooner rather than later. Others were exposed to the more subtle temptation to compromise with the customs of their pagan environment. For it was not only official repression that Christians had to expect: they incurred the enmity of society because of their reputation as "haters of the human race."[1] They won this reputation largely because, to their way of thinking, so much of contemporary pagan life was bound up with practices which they regarded as idolatrous and immoral that they could not participate in them. Just a little conformity would make conditions easier for them, and it is plain from what is said to the seven churches that such conformity was becoming acceptable in some of them.

But, whether the temptation took the form of brutal assault or social pressure, John, the writer of Revelation, insists that it must be withstood. He himself, at the time of writing, was in the Aegean island of Patmos for "the word of God and the testimony of Jesus" (Rev. 1: 9). This is traditionally, and probably with good reason, taken to mean that he had been exiled there on account of his activity. Thus he speaks of himself as sharing with his readers "in Jesus the tribulation and the kingdom and the patient endurance". His placing of "the kingdom" between "the tribulation" and "the patient endurance" underlines a recurrent New Testament theme – that the patient endurance of tribulation is the way into the kingdom of God.[2] If, then, John encourages his friends in the churches of Asia to stand firm, he is not cheering them on from the sidelines; he is involved in the same struggle. Long drawn out as the struggle may be, the issue (he assures them) is not in doubt; they are on the winning side, for Christ, their Leader, has conquered the enemy. Their only means of resisting the enemy's attack, whatever form it may take, is patient endurance and faithful confession. This may mean suffering and death; but it was precisely by suffering and death that their Leader had conquered. It is to Jesus, not to Caesar, that world dominion belongs; it is Jesus, not Caesar, who is Lord of history, and those who confess him faithfully before Caesar and Caesar's representatives participate in his victory and kingly power. As John puts it in his portrayal of the cosmic enemy in the guise of a great red dragon, the objects of his malice "conquered him by the blood of the Lamb and by the word of their testimony, for they loved not their lives even unto death" (Rev. 12: 11).

[1] One of the earliest pagan references to Christians describes them in these terms (Tacitus, *Annals* xv. 44. 5).
[2] Cf. Acts 14: 22; see also pp. 22, 47.

The chief earthly agent employed by the dragon in his assault on the church is the Roman Empire, portrayed as a seven-headed monster (like Leviathan of earlier days).[3] The monster's heads are interpreted as successive emperors; the persecuting city of Rome, economically dependent on the Empire, is depicted as a richly bedizened harlot seated on the monster, "drunk with the blood of the saints and the blood of the martyrs of Jesus" (Rev. 17:6). The Empire's hostility to the church is compounded by the growing insistence on emperor-worship. The imperial cult had long been established in the province of Asia, and however ready Christians might have been to obey the emperor in all things lawful, they could not pay him divine honours without forswearing their allegiance to Christ.[4] Conflict was inevitable, and in such a conflict the church, by all natural reckoning, was in danger of being wiped out by the power of the Empire. But the church triumphed, using just those resources recommended in the Revelation; incredible to relate, it was the Empire that at last gave way.

The Triumph of Christ

Much of the detailed symbolism in which the message of Revelation is conveyed, immediately intelligible as it may have been to those for whom it was first written, is remote and unfamiliar to readers today. But the main emphasis of the book comes through clearly: it is the book of the triumph of Christ, for his single-handed triumph on the cross and his subsequent triumph in his people's fidelity are all of a piece. Its emphasis comes through with special clarity to those who find themselves in the same kind of situation as confronted its first readers: from it they learn that, however prolonged and arduous their conflict may be, victory is theirs if they maintain their loyalty to Christ. In Oscar Cullmann's terminology, D-day guarantees

[3] In Ps. 74:14 Leviathan is said to be many-headed; that the heads were seven in number is attested in the Ugaritic text 67:1:1–3 and in *Odes of Solomon* 22:5. The dragon of Rev. 12:3 is also portrayed with seven heads.

[4] The attitude to the Roman state in Rev. 13:1ff is in marked contrast to that of Rom. 13:1–7, but now the state has exceeded the bounds of its divinely appointed ministry: Caesar is demanding the things that are God's as well as the things that are Caesar's. Or, to use the language of II Thess. 2:3ff, the restraining power has itself become the "man of lawlessness".

V-day:[5] once the decisive battle has been fought and won on the cross, the final outcome is assured. He who overcame the powers of evil there will be seen eventually to be the complete and final overcomer. The promises of ultimate glory to the overcomers in the letters to the churches and elsewhere in the book[6] are incentives to be faithful followers of him who has overcome; thus they will share his triumphal glory on the day of his manifestation. "Our Lamb has conquered; let us follow him."

The City of God

John's last vision, the vision of the New Jerusalem, looks forward to the consummation of the divine purpose of blessing for the world. The New Jerusalem, the city of God, is the community of believers, the glorified church. As in Ephesians the church is an advance model of the reconciled universe yet to be, so in Revelation the church is a blessing to the purified and renovated earth.[7] In it God dwells among men and extends his covenant worldwide, for "they shall be his peoples,[8] and God himself will be with them and be their God" (Rev. 21: 3). This is the ancient language of covenant, once restricted to a particular community but now unconfined in its range.

The biblical themes of covenant and election have been strangely misunderstood by some theologians, who have thought that if some are chosen by God, it means that others are left outside the scope of his grace. The truth is different: if some are chosen by God, it is in order that others through them may be brought within the scope of his grace. This was so with Israel among the nations; it is so with the church in the world. "You are the light of the world", said Jesus

[5] *Christ and Time*, E.T. (London, 1951), p. 141: while "the 'Victory Day' does in fact present *something new* in contrast to the decisive battle already fought", yet "this new thing that the 'Victory Day' brings is based entirely upon that decisive battle, and would be absolutely impossible without it."

[6] Rev. 2: 7, 11, 17, 26ff; 3: 5, 12, 21; also 21: 7.

[7] The new heaven and new earth of Rev. 21: 1 are the fulfilment of the divine promise of Isa. 65: 17 (cf. 66: 22) – a passage echoed also in II Peter 3: 13 (see p. 95).

[8] The plural "peoples" is a more probable reading here than the singular "people"; the scribal tendency was to alter the plural to the more familiar singular.

to his disciples (Matt. 5: 14); using the same figure John in theRevelation says of the perfected church: "By its light shall the nations walk" (Rev. 21: 24). But they can walk by its light only if its light has been preserved undimmed.

Nine

The Church in the World

The Message of the General Letters

THERE IS A PERVASIVE AMBIVALENCE THROUGHOUT THE NEW Testament writings wherever the church's attitude to the world in which it exists comes to expression. On the one hand, the world is God's world, created by God and loved by God, currently alienated from God, it is true, but destined to be redeemed and reconciled to God. On the other hand, the world is dominated by a spirit totally opposed to God, organized in such a way as to exclude God, drawn towards unworthy goals of material status and self-interest, quite different from the goals towards which the Christian way leads. In this latter aspect the world is, according to the NEB rendering, "the godless world", as when John writes in his first letter: "Do not set your hearts on the godless world or anything in it. Anyone who loves the world is a stranger to the Father's love. Everything the world affords, all that panders to the appetites or entices the eyes, all the glamour of its life, springs not from the Father but from the godless world. And that world is passing away with all its allurements, but he who does God's will stands for evermore" (I John 2: 15–17).

The Christian is sent into the godless world to reclaim it for its rightful Lord,[1] but while it remains the "godless world" it is an uncongenial environment for the Christian; he cannot feel at home there. When the writer to the Hebrews says that the patriarchs of Israel "acknowledged that they were strangers and exiles on the earth" because their true homeland was elsewhere (Heb. 11: 13), he recommends their attitude as one which his readers should imitate.

This emphasis on being in the world but not of it, involved and

[1] See p. 85.

detached at the same time, can be found in many parts of the New Testament, but not least in those documents which are traditionally called the "catholic" or "general" letters, because they are addressed not to specific churches or individuals but to a wider and more indefinite circle of readers.

The Letter of James

The Letter of James, for example, is addressed to "the twelve tribes in the Dispersion". The "Dispersion" (*diaspora*) commonly denoted the large number of Jews who lived among the Gentiles outside Palestine – in the Roman provinces to the west or in the Parthian Empire farther east. But the "Dispersion" to which James writes is a Christian dispersion, Jewish-Christian perhaps but none the less certainly Christian. He designates himself as "a servant of God and of the Lord Jesus Christ"; his readers, like himself, "hold the faith of our Lord Jesus Christ, the Lord of glory" – or perhaps we should read "the Lord Jesus Christ, our glory" (Jas. 2: 1)[2] – while the "honourable name" by which they are called (2: 7) can be no other than the name of Jesus.

The Letter of James has been saddled for four and a half centuries with the disparaging description first given to it by Luther: "a right strawy epistle".[3] But the New Testament would be poorer without it. It insists in downright terms that Christian faith, if it is to be worthy of the name, must be shown in Christian practice. The mere profession of belief in God is useless if a man's actions do not match his profession. Faith without works is dead, James declares – and he declares it in language which suggests that he has in mind certain perversions of Paul's gospel of justification by faith which Paul also denounces (Jas. 2: 14ff). Faith in Christ is incompatible with social snobbery or a quarrelsome spirit. The spirit of Zealot intolerance was increasing in Palestine when James wrote, as well as in the Jewish communities elsewhere, and he warns his readers not to become infected by it. "Jealousy and selfish ambition" have nothing in

[2] Or Jesus may be called absolutely "the glory" – the divine *shekinah* resident in a human life, as in John 1: 14 (see p. 105).
[3] Preface to New Testament translation (Weimar edition 6, p. 39); cf. Preface to Epistle of James (Weimar edition 7, pp. 384ff).

common with "the wisdom from above", which is "first pure, then peaceable, gentle, open to reason, full of mercy and good fruits, without uncertainty or insincerity" (Jas. 3: 14–17). In these last words James portrays the Christian character, and he may even be portraying a character which he had seen lived out at close quarters – the character of him whom in later years he came to recognize as the wisdom of God in a human life.

But James, who in several places echoes the Sermon on the Mount, can flay the rich oppressors of his people with the vehemence of an Old Testament prophet. The denunciation of the wealthy landowners and the prediction of their impending ruin in Jas. 5: 1–6 are reminiscent of Amos's invective against those who in his day "sold the righteous for silver and the needy for a pair of shoes" (Amos 2: 6). If James wrote against a Palestinian background, his prediction was amply fulfilled in the economic disaster which befell the chief-priestly and Sadducean aristocracy as a result of the revolt against Rome in A.D. 66. But to his readers the impending catastrophe was a sign that liberation was at hand: "Be patient, therefore, brethren, until the coming of the Lord" (5: 7).

The First Letter of Peter

The "Dispersion" motif appears also in the opening salutation of I Peter – addressed "to the exiles of the Dispersion" in five provinces of Asia Minor, who later in this letter are described as "aliens and exiles" (2: 11). Here too it is a Christian "dispersion" that is in view, but a "dispersion" comprising converts from paganism.

The greater part of I Peter helps the readers to understand how Christians ought to live in a world which does not provide congenial soil for the cultivation of Christian graces. Indeed, it has been held by several students of the letter that I Peter 1: 3–4: 11 bears the marks of an exhortation to new converts on the occasion of their baptism. They have not yet reached the maturity which requires to be sustained by solid food but are encouraged to acquire an appetite for "the pure spiritual milk, that by it you may grow up to salvation" (2: 2). When the meaning of baptism is expounded in 3: 21f, it is mentioned as something which they are experiencing "now". They are now followers of the risen Christ, "who has gone into heaven and is at the right hand of God, with angels, authorities and powers subject to him" (probably a fragment of a primitive baptismal confession). They are entering a new society, which is described in Old Testament idiom as "a chosen race, a royal priesthood, a holy nation, God's own people" (2: 9). They are "living stones" in a spiritual temple, bonded together by the "cornerstone chosen and precious" foretold by Isaiah and fulfilled in Christ; to change the figure, they are members of the "holy priesthood" in this new temple, offering up "spiritual sacrifices acceptable to God through Jesus Christ" (2: 4–6).[4] They must bid farewell to pagan vices and put on Christian virtues. As the nation of Israel in earlier days was called to be holy because its God was holy, so to them now comes the divine command: "You shall be holy, for I am holy" (I Peter 1: 16, quoting Lev. 11: 44f). They must maintain good conduct among their pagan neighbours, and when surprise is expressed that they no longer join their old companions in the "wild profligacy" in which they once indulged, they must be ready with a reply, given with gentleness and respect, to those who call them to account for their new-found hope (3: 15).

This exhortation to the Christian way is not confined to generalities; it descends to particular situations of social and domestic life, including, for example, advice to a Christian wife married to a pagan husband and to Christian slaves serving pagan masters (2: 18–3: 6). Christians were given a bad name throughout the Roman world as subversive agitators; let them see to it that their behaviour gave the lie to such calumnies. "Honour all men. Love the brotherhood. Fear God. Honour the emperor" (2: 17).

In this part of I Peter it is recognized that suffering may well be a Christian's lot. Christ himself suffered, and if his people are called upon to suffer for him, let them "arm themselves" with his mind (4: 1). Persecution, however, is viewed as a remote contingency: "who is there to harm you if you are zealous for what is right? But even if you should suffer for righteousness' sake, you will be blessed" (3: 13f). The important thing is that, if they did suffer, it should be "for doing right, if that should be God's will", and not for doing wrong (3: 17). But after the doxology which concludes the first part of the document comes a further passage which has the nature of a

[4] See p. 79.

letter of encouragement in face of persecution. Far from being a remote contingency, suffering for their faith at the hands of the authorities is now an imminent certainty. A "fiery ordeal" is coming to test them, and they must not be dismayed or discouraged, "but rejoice", they are told, "in so far as you share Christ's sufferings, that you may also rejoice and be glad when his glory is revealed" (4: 12f). To suffer for criminal activity would be disgraceful, but to be "reproached for the name of Christ" is an honour: "if one suffers as a Christian, let him not be ashamed, but under that name let him glorify God" (4: 14–16).

Thus in 1 Peter we can see the imperial attitude to the church changing before our eyes. Persecution for the name of Christ has broken out at Rome, and it will soon reach the Christians of Asia Minor, who accordingly are here being alerted to its imminence.[5] The leaders of the Christian communities would be the first targets of attack, and hence they are given a special word of encouragement: Peter addresses them "as a fellow elder and a witness of the sufferings of Christ as well as a partaker of the glory that is to be revealed" (5: 1). They are not alone in exposure to persecution: "the same experience of suffering is required of your brotherhood throughout the world; and after you have suffered a little while, the God of all grace, who has called you to his eternal glory in Christ, will himself restore, establish, and strengthen you" (5: 9f).

The Letters of Jude and Second Peter

The churches were faced with internal dangers as well as dangers from the outside world, and some of the "general letters" were written to counter such internal dangers. In Acts 20: 29f Paul, in his farewell speech to the elders of the Ephesian church, warns them that "fierce wolves will come in among you, not sparing the flock; and from among your own selves will arise men speaking perverse things, to draw away the disciples after them." The later New Testament writings show how true a forecast this was, and not only at Ephesus. The letters of Jude and II Peter (which incorporates much of Jude) warn Christians in general against such teachers of error. Their error concerned morals as much as doctrine, for they are placed in

[5] Cf. the setting of Revelation (see pp. 84ff).

the succession of the fallen angels who courted "the daughters of men" in antediluvian days,[6] of the men of Sodom and of the Israelites who perished in the wilderness because they fell into idolatry and immorality.[7] To Paul's indignant question, "Are we to continue in sin that grace may abound?" (Rom. 6: 1), they would have returned a confident "Yes!" But the doom of these "ungodly persons who pervert the grace of our God into licentiousness" (Jude 4) was foretold by the prophets and reaffirmed by the apostles; Christians must therefore avoid them, while doing all they can to rescue those whom they had led astray, and make sure that they themselves are firmly established in the faith by perseverance in prayer, love and hope.

In II Peter the exposure of these "loud-mouthed boasters" is preceded by a positive insistence on the validity of the apostolic witness to "the power and coming of our Lord Jesus Christ" (a witness based on personal experience), by which the writings of the prophets are confirmed. The united testimony of prophets and apostles, illuminated by the Spirit under whose impulse "men spoke from God", should serve believers as "a lamp shining in a dark place, until the day dawns and the morning star rises in your hearts" (II Pet. 1: 16–21). Thus they would be protected against the temptation to follow false guides.

Another question which is dealt with in II Peter is one which has left its mark in various parts of the New Testament, but nowhere so explicitly as here: the problem of the postponed advent. For those who expected Christ's advent within the lifetime of the first Christian generation its non-arrival constituted a problem, to which indeed some found ready solutions by way of reinterpretation and the like. But others dismissed the whole idea as a delusion: "Where", they asked, "is the promise of his coming? For ever since the fathers fell asleep, all things have continued as they were from the beginning of creation" (II Peter 3: 4). To this question three answers are given in II Peter:

(*a*) The present continuity of normal existence will not endure indefinitely. There is precedent for a cataclysm disrupting the order of nature in the flood of Noah's day. As then water was the means of

[6] Gen. 6: 1ff.
[7] The precedent of the wilderness wanderings is repeatedly adduced for ethical lessons in the New Testament; cf. 1 Cor. 10: 1ff; Heb. 3: 7ff, as well as Jude 5.

destroying the old world, so it will be "the fire next time". When at last the day of the Lord comes "like a thief" (a recurring New Testament simile),[8] "the heavens will be kindled and dissolved, and the elements will melt with fire", to be replaced by "new heavens and a new earth in which righteousness dwells" (3: 10–13).[9]

(*b*) God is not limited to the time-scale of human life on earth. It is wise to remember the psalmist's words:

> A thousand ages in thy sight
> Are like an evening gone,
> Short as the watch that ends the night
> Before the rising sun.[10]

What is one brief generation to him with whom "one day is as a thousand years, and a thousand years as one day" (3: 8)?

(*c*) If the advent is postponed, it is because God in his mercy is deferring the day of wrath; as Paul had said, God's forbearance is man's salvation.[11] "The Lord is not slow about his promise as some count slowness, but is forbearing towards you, not wishing that any should perish, but that all should reach repentance" (3: 9).

Hence, the call to Christians is to be on their guard against being swept from their foundations by hope deferred, but rather, by holy living, to look forward to and even to speed the coming of the day of God and to "grow in the grace and knowledge of our Lord and Saviour Jesus Christ" (3: 11f, 17f).

The First Letter of John

The most penetrating and valuable of the general letters is that traditionally entitled the First Letter of John,[12] because it is concerned with a central and permanent issue – the relevance of the person of Christ to the Christian faith. It was called forth by a

---

[8] Cf. Matt. 24: 43//Luke 12: 39; I Thess. 5: 2, 4; Rev. 16: 15.

[9] From Isa. 65: 17 (66: 22); cf. Rev. 21: 1ff (see p. 87).

[10] Isaac Watts' paraphrase of Psalm 90: 4.

[11] A reference perhaps to Rom. 2: 4, "Do you not know that God's kindness is meant to lead you to repentence?"

[12] II John and III John are not general letters but have particular destinations. II John especially the message of I John is applied to a local situation.

division in a circle of Christian communities, probably in the province of Asia: an élitist group, claiming to have found the secret of eternal life in an advanced form of teaching, had seceded from their former associates who maintained the Christian message which they had "heard from the beginning"[13] – a message which they could not reconcile with the new teaching of the seceders. John, as one who had known the Christian way "from the beginning", wrote to reassure those who remained true to the original message that it was they, and not the others, who had eternal life. For eternal life was embodied in the person of Christ, in whom the recipients of the letter continued to place their faith, whereas the Christ whom the seceders professed was no true Christ at all.

As far as can be gathered, the seceders appear to have embraced a view similar to that of Cerinthus, a gnostic leader of this very period, according to whom the "Christ" was a spirit-being which came upon the man Jesus of Nazareth at his baptism enabling him to accomplish his works of power, but left him before his death.[14] Thus they dehistoricized essential Christianity, forcing a division between the Jesus of history and the Christ of faith. John will not hear of such a division: "Every one who believes that Jesus is the Christ is a child of God", he says (I John 5: 1), with the implied corollary that no one who denies the identity of Jesus with the Christ can claim to be a member of God's family or to have any share in eternal life (which is only to be had within God's family). Even if such a denial were voiced by a prophetic spirit, no matter: "every spirit which confesses that Jesus Christ has come in the flesh is of God, and every spirit which disunites Jesus[15] [disunites the genuinely human Jesus from the Christ of faith] is not of God; this is the spirit of antichrist" (I John 4: 2f). The depreciation of the material order as devoid of religious relevance struck at the root of every Christian foundation – creation and resurrection as well as incarnation.

[13] Cf. I John 2: 24 (this may be the sense of "that which was from the beginning" in I John 1: 1).

[14] Irenaeus, *Against Heresies* i. 26. 1.

[15] Cf. R. A. Knox's translation: "no spirit which would disunite Jesus comes from God". On the principle that the more difficult reading is to be preferred, this has claims to be regarded as more original than "every spirit which does not confess Jesus is not of God" (which may represent an early attempt to interpret the more difficult reading).

It may be in refutation of the Cerinthian reconstruction of the gospel story that John says so emphatically that Jesus Christ, one indissoluble being, "came by water and blood . . . not with the water only but with the water and the blood" (I John 5: 6). Whatever further significance the water and the blood may have, they denote primarily Jesus' baptism in Jordan and his death on the cross. The divine power was as truly manifested on the cross as at the baptism; there was no question of its coming on Jesus when he was baptized but leaving him before he died. The death of Jesus fixes him in history; he who died was a real man of flesh – and blood. But at the same time that death has abiding significance: for those who remain in the fellowship of God by walking in his light "the blood of Jesus his Son provides cleansing from all sin" (I John 1: 7). He who died is now their "advocate with the Father, Jesus Christ the righteous" (I John 2: 1)[16] – Jesus the Christ, indissoluble now in exaltation as formerly on earth. His advocacy provides the assurance of pardon and cleansing for his people's sins – "and not for ours only", John adds, "but also for the whole world" (2: 2).

> He ever lives above
>   For me to intercede,
> His all-redeeming love,
>   His precious blood, to plead;
> His blood atoned for all our race
> And sprinkles now the throne of grace.[17]

But the seceders were not dismayed by being told that this atoning efficacy was not available to those who severed themselves from the fellowship of believers in the indissoluble Jesus Christ. They needed no such atonement because, they claimed, they had no sin (I John 1: 8); they had reached a stage of spiritual progress where "merely" ethical distinctions were irrelevant. With their new theology they combined a new morality. But their new morality was defective not only because of its denial of the need for cleansing from sin, but also because it paid scant attention to the paramount claims of love. Like the "men of the Spirit" at Corinth with whom Paul had to take issue (I Cor. 8: 1), they rated knowledge far above love. Hence John

[16] See p. 76.
[17] C. Wesley.

repeatedly emphasizes the all-surpassing exigency of Christ's commandment of love. Love to God cannot be seen except in love to man, and love to man must express itself in acts of love. There is no incompatibility between love and obedience: love to God will be manifested in obedience to his commandments, and the chief of his commandments is that his children should love one another. If they do not, they are not his children. Love is an infallible and indispensable criterion of the presence of eternal life. Eternal life will be found in the fellowship of those who love one another.

The restatement of the gospel in a new idiom is necessary in every generation – as necessary as its translation into new languages. If the author of this letter is the author of the Fourth Gospel (which is most probable), then he himself performed a most valuable service when he restated the gospel in a new idiom towards the end of the first Christian century. But it was the unimpaired gospel that he restated.[18] In too much that passes for restatement of the gospel the gospel itself disappears, and the resultant product is what Paul would have called "another gospel which is in fact no gospel at all" (Gal. 1: 6f). When the Christian message is so thoroughly accommodated to the prevalent climate of opinion that it becomes one more expression of that climate of opinion, it is no longer the Christian message. The Christian message must address itself in judgment and mercy to the prevalent climate of opinion, and can do so only when it is distinct from it. If it fails to do so, it has succumbed to that godless worldliness against which John warns his readers. The new teaching which the other party cultivated was guilty of precisely this: it adapted the Christian message so completely to current movements of gnostic thought that it became one among other expressions of that thought and lost its Christian content. Then, when gnostic thought of that order became obsolete, this "restatement" became obsolete with it, whereas the message which was "from the beginning" has survived and retains its power today.

John's readers, anointed by the Holy Spirit, were initiated into the true knowledge (2: 20); they had a built-in instinct which enabled them to detect religious error when it was presented to them under the guise of truth. "I write this to you who believe in the name of the Son of God", he says, "that you may know that you have eternal

[18] See pp. 100.

life" (5: 13). In the historical Jesus in whom they had placed their faith they had found "the true God and eternal life" (5: 20); therefore, he concludes, "little children, keep yourselves from idols" (5: 21). In other words, seeing you have come to know the truth, beware of imitations and refuse all substitutes.

Ten

The Word Became Flesh

The Message of the Gospel of John

BY THE LAST DECADE OF THE FIRST CENTURY A.D. THE CHRISTIAN centre of gravity had shifted a long way from Jerusalem, where it was located in the period immediately following the death and resurrection of Jesus: it was now to be found in the regions bordering on the Aegean Sea. This shift was due largely to Paul's missionary activity in the middle years of the century, but throughout the main period of Paul's activity the influence of Jerusalem remained unimpaired. While Paul maintained that his apostolic ministry was entirely independent of any commission or authorization from the leaders of the Jerusalem church, he nevertheless attached great importance to preserving close fellowship with them and endeavoured to foster this fellowship by organizing a fund in the churches of his Aegean mission-field for the relief of the Jerusalem church. Indeed, Paul was a better friend to Jerusalem than Jerusalem was to him, for he taught his converts to look on the believing community there as the mother-church of Christendom and brought non-Jerusalemite versions of the gospel into line with that which he and the Jerusalem leaders held in common.[1]

The Setting of John's Gospel

Yet a few years after Paul's death the Jerusalem church was dispersed and the city itself lay in ruins. Jewish Christianity became increasingly a backwater as compared with what was now the main stream of Gentile Christianity. To a new Christian generation growing up in

[1] Cf. Acts 19: 1–7.

the Aegean world late in the century Jerusalem and Palestine were not only geographically remote but the way of life which had been current there before A.D. 70 and which formed the setting of the gospel narrative belonged to another world – one which, they felt, had passed away for ever. In any case, it was asked, did it matter *where* the gospel narrative had its setting? Indeed, did it matter *when* the events which it recorded took place? The climate of opinion by which this generation had its thinking moulded was not greatly concerned about historical fact: eternal truth was the important thing. Historical fact was tied to time and place and subject to the "scandal of particularity"; an insistence on historical fact obscured the universal relevance of eternal truth.

The prevalent climate of opinion, moreover, tended to elevate the concept of spirit and depreciate the material order. Eternal truth belonged to the spiritual realm; historical fact was too closely tied to the material order. Reflexion on the primitive gospel story in the light of this trend of thought was prone to dehistoricize it and modify it in other ways. The primitive story had centred around a historical individual, Jesus of Nazareth, who had lived in the first thirty years of the century, and it ascribed saving efficacy to his death. True, the story went on to tell how he had been raised from the dead and exalted as universal Lord; but would it not be better to concentrate on the universal Lord, who belonged to the spiritual realm, and lay less stress on the earlier phase of his existence as Jesus of Nazareth? Or, in so far as that earlier phase had to be reckoned with, might one not think of a spiritual being assuming the appearance of humanity, rather than of a real man of woman born, a man of flesh and blood? If a spiritual being wished to reveal eternal truth to mankind, he might well take on human appearance in order to do so, without really becoming man.

This line of argument was bound to lead men and women far afield from the primitive story of Jesus, localized and attached to a historical context as it was; we can see where it might lead if we look at some of the Gnostic systems of the second century, which have little enough in common with the picture that Mark paints of the Galilaean ministry. If the message of Mark and the Gnostic systems could equally be called Christian, then wherein, it might be asked, does essential Christianity consist?

It was in this changing situation at the end of the first century that the work which we call the Gospel of John made its appearance. Its great contribution to Christian life and thought was its demonstration that the eternal truth of the gospel could be maintained without detriment to its historical factuality. On the one hand, it remains true to the main emphases of the primitive preaching. Jesus engages in a three years' ministry of teaching and action in Judaea, Samaria and Galilee. True, Judaea (especially Jerusalem) plays a predominant part in this Gospel, the author of which, someone has said, knows his Jerusalem (knows it from memory, as it stood before its destruction) "as a Euston taxi-driver knows his London."[2] In the Synoptic account, on the other hand, Judaea and Jerusalem provide the scene of the passion narrative; but John's record preserves a "tradition" of the ministry independent of those which the Synoptic evangelists preserve. Yet in John's account, as in theirs, Jesus is crucified by sentence of Pilate, the Roman governor of Judaea, and the charge on which he was convicted is summed up in the words "The King of the Jews" inscribed on the placard fixed to the cross.[3] For John, as for his predecessors, the events which reveal God and bring his salvation near to mankind are events which happened once for all.

But in these events, John insists, fixed as they are in time and place, eternal truth is uniquely unfolded. That this is so he shows in the course of his narrative, largely by means of the teaching of Jesus in which the significance of the events is brought out. That this is so he also shows in another way in the prologue to his work, when he affirms that Jesus, the one of whom these events are narrated, is the embodiment of eternal truth. In his ministry eternal truth was concentrated into a limited measure of space and time, that men might grasp and believe it; in Jesus himself, we might say (translating John's language into an idiom of today) eternal truth was "earthed". Far from a spiritual being's taking on but the outward appearance of humanity, in Jesus eternal truth "became flesh"[4] and took up residence among men.

[2] A. R. Short, *The Bible and Modern Medicine* (London, 1931), p. 178.
[3] See p. 110.
[4] John 1: 14.

Word and Wisdom

To express the concept of eternal truth John uses the Greek term *logos*, which most of our English versions render "word". "In the beginning was the Word", he says, "and the Word was with God, and the Word was God. He was in the beginning with God; all things were made through him, and without him was not anything made that was made" (John 1: 1–3).

The word *logos* was a current term in Greek philosophy to denote the rational principle in man and, on a cosmic scale, the universal principle which imposed order on the raw material of which the world was made. When Christianity spread into the more intellectual areas of the Graeco-Roman world, it was natural that the use of *logos* in John's prologue should be understood in this sense. Thus the Christian philosopher Justin Martyr, in the middle of the second century, argued that men like Socrates, who cultivated true reason before Christ's coming, were in a sense Christians before Christ, since they lived in conformity with *logos*.[5] The word thus became a bridge-term by which Christianity passed from one culture to another.

But the background of John's terminology is properly to be sought in the Old Testament, where the "word" of Yahweh is his will in action. If "in the beginning" God spoke the world and its contents into being, from the moment when "God said, 'Let there be light'" to the moment when "God said, 'Let us make man . . .'" (Gen. 1: 1–26), it could be said that he created all things by his "word". So Psalm 33: 6 puts it:

> By the word of the LORD the heavens were made,
> and all their host by the breath of his mouth.

Or when God made his purpose known to his people through one of his spokesmen the prophets, the prophet might say "Thus says the LORD" (e.g. Amos 1: 3) or he might say, more vividly, "The word of the LORD came to me" (e.g. Jer. 1: 4). The "word of the LORD" is spoken of almost as though it were a divine messenger or agent (e.g. Isa. 55: 11):

---

[5] *First Apology* 5: 3ff; 46: 3ff.

> my word . . . that goes forth from my mouth . . .
>   shall not return to me empty,
> but it shall accomplish that which I purpose,
>   and prosper in the thing for which I sent it.

This purpose may be the help and deliverance of those who call to God in their need (e.g. Ps. 107: 20):

> he sent forth his word, and healed them,
>   and delivered them from destruction.

Or it may be a work of judgment, as in a well-known passage in the Book of Wisdom (18: 15f) which describes Egypt's visitation by the angel of death on the first passover night:

> Thy all-powerful word leaped from heaven, from the royal throne,
>   into the midst of the land that was doomed,
> a stern warrior carrying the sharp sword of thy authentic command,
> and stood and filled all things with death,
> and touched heaven while standing on the earth.

Alongside this personification of the *word* of God we can trace a parallel personification of his *wisdom*, notably in the works which we know as Israel's "wisdom literature" and pre-eminently in Prov. 8: 22–31, where Wisdom speaks in the first person as the eldest daughter of the Creator, who was with him when he made the universe:

> The LORD created me at the beginning of his work,
>   the first of his acts of old. . . .
> When he established the heavens, I was there . . .
>   when he marked out the foundations of the earth,
> then I was beside him, like a master workman;
>   and I was daily his delight,
>   rejoicing before him always,
> rejoicing in his inhabited world
>   and delighting in the sons of men.

This may in origin be little more than a poetical way of saying what has been said more prosaically a few chapters earlier, in Prov. 3: 19:

> The LORD by wisdom founded the earth;
> by understanding he established the heavens –

but put in this form it provided a ready-made idiom for those early Christian thinkers who recognized in Jesus the *personal* and not merely *personified* word and wisdom of God.[6] The plural "thinkers" is deliberate, for this recognition is not peculiar to the Gospel of John: it is found independently in Paul's writings (cf. Col. 1: 15–17), in Hebrews (Heb. 1: 1–3) and in the Apocalypse (Rev. 3: 14). But it is in the Johannine prologue that it receives classic expression. When we read that the Word "was in the beginning with God" (John 1: 3), it is easy to detect the echo of the language of Wisdom who, "at the beginning of his work . . . was beside him" (Prov. 8: 22, 30). Only, unlike personified Wisdom, the personal Word is uncreated, not only enjoying the divine companionship but sharing the divine essence.

The Incarnate Glory

All the self-revealing ways in which God acted in earlier days, when he sent forth his word, says John, are summed up and transcended in Jesus, for in him "the Word became flesh and dwelt among us, and we have beheld his glory . . . full of grace and truth" (John 1: 14). The divine presence which dwelt among the tribes of Israel and was manifested by the unapproachable glory in the Mosaic tabernacle and in Solomon's temple (Ex. 25: 8; 40: 34; I Kings 8: 10f) has now come to earth in a human life. As Paul in II Cor. 3: 7–4: 6 draws a contrast between the fading glory on Moses' face and the unfading glory in the face of Christ, so John implies a contrast between the full revelation of glory which he and his companions had seen and the partial revelation once granted to Moses. Moses prayed that he might see the divine glory but was told that he could see only its afterglow – "for", said God, "man shall not see me and live" (Ex. 33: 20). But as the divine "goodness" passed before him, the meaning of the ineffable name was pronounced in his hearing: "Yahweh, a God compassionate and merciful, slow to anger, and abounding in grace and truth" (Ex. 34: 6). The full glory that was

[6] See pp. 34f.

veiled from Moses' eyes was perceived by those with whom the incarnate Word took up his abode; the God whom man could not see and live was seen in him, that men might live: "No one has ever seen God; the only-begotten who has his being in the Father's bosom is the one who has made him known" (John 1: 18). In Jesus the glory of God has come down to earth, full of grace and truth; now read on, says John in effect, and see how it was manifested.

After the prologue the term "the Word" is not used again in the Gospel in this personal sense, but the prologue shows how the story which follows is to be understood. Indeed, the sequence of thought in the prologue is repeated at length in the main part of the Gospel. The Divine Word active in the old creation (John 1: 3) appears as the agent of the new creation in chapters 1 to 4; the Word in whom was life (1: 4a) appears as the life of mankind in chapters 5 and 6; the light which shone unvanquished amid the darkness (1: 4b, 5, 9) appears as the light of the world in chapters 7 to 9.

As the word of God came to Israel in many forms of mighty act and prophetic utterance, so the consummating revelation in Christ is depicted throughout the Gospel under a wealth of imagery drawn from the Old Testament – the water of life,[7] the bread of life,[8] the light of life,[9] the serpent on the pole,[10] the passover lamb,[11] and so forth.

Again, as the living Word was rejected by "his own people" when he came "to his own home" (1: 11), so in chapters 10 to 12 Christ is disowned by those who should have welcomed him: "though he had done so many signs before them, yet they did not believe in him" (12: 37). But as in the prologue "to all who received him . . . he gave power to become children of God" (1: 12), so in the upper room discourse and intercession before the passion (chapters 13–17) and in the resurrection appearances afterwards (chapters 20, 21) Christ communicates his love without reserve to those who are "his own people" in fact and not merely in name, and faith triumphs over doubt in Thomas's adoring confession: "My Lord and my God" (20: 28). And as in the prologue the evangelist testifies how he and

[7] John 4: 10ff; 7: 37ff.
[8] John 6: 32ff.
[9] John 8: 12; cf. 1: 9; 3: 19–21; 9: 5; 12: 46.
[10] John 3: 14f.
[11] John 1: 29; 19: 36.

his associates beheld the glory of the Word become flesh (1: 14), so in the succession of "signs" recorded in the Gospel that glory is revealed. In the first of his signs at Cana, Jesus "manifested his glory" in a manner that aroused faith in his disciples (2: 11), and in the last sign before the passion, the raising of Lazarus from death, the believing witnesses saw "the glory of God" (11: 40).

But in this Gospel the supreme manifestation of the glory of God takes place at the cross; Isaac Watts caught the evangelist's thought well when he sang:

> But in the grace that rescued man
> His brightest form of glory shines;
> Here, on the cross, 'tis fairest drawn,
> In precious blood, and crimson lines.

With a characteristic *double entendre*, Jesus' being "lifted up" on the cross is his being "lifted up" in glory, that all may be drawn to him and recognize him for what he truly is (John 8: 28; 12: 32); it was there that "the hour came for the Son of man to be glorified" (12: 23).

Signs and Discourses

What are elsewhere described as the miracles or mighty works of Jesus are by John called his "signs" because the eye of faith could penetrate beyond the outward act and discern what it signified – the embodiment of the divine glory in "Jesus of Nazareth, the son of Joseph", as men called him (1: 45). Chief among the signs are the changing of the water into wine (2: 1–11), the healing of the nobleman's son (4: 46–54), the healing of the cripple at the pool of Bethesda (5: 1–15), the feeding of the five thousand (6: 1–14), the imparting of sight to the man born blind (9: 1–38) and the raising of Lazarus, a sign of the truth that Jesus is "the resurrection and the life" (11: 1–44).

In addition to his recording of these signs, John conveys his message also in a succession of discourses spoken by Jesus, beginning with his words to Nicodemus about the new birth (3: 1–15) and his conversation with the Samaritan woman about the water of life (4: 1–26). Sometimes the discourse is appended to a "sign" so as to bring out its meaning.

107

When Mark describes the feeding of the five thousand, for example, he gives us the impression that there was more in the incident than met the eye – more than the disciples themselves could grasp. "They did not understand about the loaves", says Mark, "but their hearts were hardened" (Mark 6: 52) – that is, their power of comprehension was obscured. But what is only hinted at in Mark is brought into the open by John, for after his straightforward narration of the feeding, he provides its interpretation in the discourse delivered by Jesus in the Capernaum synagogue. The material bread was but a symbol of the true bread from heaven –

> the holy bread
> By which the soul of man is fed –

which, unlike the manna in the wilderness, enables those who partake of it to live for ever. Better still: Jesus himself is the heavenly bread: "I am the bread of life; he who comes to me shall not hunger, and he who believes in me shall never thirst" (John 6: 35).

The consummating "sign", the lifting up of the Son of Man on the cross, has its significance unfolded in the upper room discourse and high-priestly prayer which precede it. Here it is revealed that the glory which shines most brightly in the passion is the glory of self-giving love. Not only so, but it is through this love, proceeding from God, embodied in Christ, and calling forth in those who receive it a responsive love to God and to one another, that believers are brought into union with God. "A new commandment I give to you", says Jesus in the upper room, "that you love one another; even as I have loved you, that you also love one another . . . If a man loves me, he will keep my word, and my Father will love him, and we will come to him and make our home with him . . . As the Father has loved me, so have I loved you; abide in my love" (John 13: 34; 14: 23; 15: 9).

C. H. Dodd insists that love is, "as a matter of fact, the only kind of union *between persons* of which we can have any possible experience", and points out that, according to John, this is the nature of the union into which God brings his people.

> He makes use of the strongest expressions for union with God that contemporary religious language provided, in order to assure his

readers that he does really mean what he says: that through faith in Christ we may enter into a personal community of life with the eternal God, which has the character of *agapē*, which is essentially supernatural and not of this world, and yet plants its feet firmly in this world, not only because real *agapē* cannot but express itself in practical conduct, but also because the crucial act of *agapē* was actually performed in history, on an April day about A.D. 30, at a supper-table in Jerusalem, in a garden across the Kidron valley, in the headquarters of Pontius Pilate, and on a Roman cross at Gologotha. So concrete, so actual, is the nature of the divine *agapē*; yet none the less for that, by entering into the relation of *agapē* thus opened up for men, we may dwell in God and He in us.[12]

It is not by accident that the upper-room discourse, in which this dominant theme recurs, provides the setting for the Paraclete-sayings, in which Jesus promises the disciples that after his departure he will send them his personal *alter ego* (John 14: 16f, 26; 15: 26f; 16: 7–15). This *alter ego*, "the Spirit of truth", will maintain the permanent presence of divine love with them and in them, in addition to his further ministries of showing them the inward meaning of Jesus' teaching, guiding them into all the truth, bearing witness to Jesus with and through their own witness, and bringing home to the world "where wrong and right and judgment lie" (16: 8, NEB).

John's story of Jesus

Our author might have composed an extended theological meditation on the revelation of divine glory and love, grace and truth, life and judgment in the ministry of Jesus. But instead of doing that, he wrote a Gospel; that is to say, he narrated the story of Jesus, and narrated it in such a way that he remained faithful to the outline of early Christian preaching and at the same time conveyed the essence of that preaching in an idiom intelligible to the reading public which he had in mind.

So far as the outline of the early preaching is concerned, he begins with the ministry of John the Baptist (although in this Gospel John is not distinguished as "the Baptist"), emphasizing John's rôle as

---

[12] *The Interpretation of the Fourth Gospel* (Cambridge, 1953), pp. 199f.

a witness. So important in his eyes was John's witness that he dove-tails its beginnings into his prologue, telling how John was sent by God as a witness to him who was the true "light of men" (John 1: 6–8). Then we are told of Jesus' own ministry in Galilee and Judaea, with a brief but fruitful Samaritan phase; the record preserved in this Gospel has more to say of Jesus' southern ministry than the Synoptic records tell. The main Galilaean episode related in this Gospel is the feeding of the five thousand; in describing it, John mentions something which throws light on the Synoptic narrative – the attempt by the enthusiastic multitude to compel Jesus to become their king (6: 15). But with Jesus' last visit to Jerusalem John's narrative proceeds more or less *pari passu* with that of the Synoptists, albeit with its own distinctive contributions and emphases, through the days of teaching in the temple to the Last Supper, the arrest, the Jewish and Roman trials, the scourging and crucifying – and then the resurrection.

The permanent meaning of this last narrative is unfolded not only in the upper room discourse and high-priestly prayer, but in occasional episodes which disclose its inwardness. Readers might think that Jesus' conviction as "the king of the Jews" – the words inscribed on the cross – concerned a local and temporary question of political allegiance. But John shows Jesus pointing out to Pilate the true nature of the kingship which he claimed – not a wordly kingship of which Roman law might take cognizance, but the kingship of truth: Jesus' willing subjects are those who are on the side of truth (John 18: 33–38). Pilate might dismiss the subject with his "What is truth?" – but more thoughtful people would realize that the answer to his question was never so close to him as it was then. If eternal truth was embodied in Jesus, could anything be more permanently and urgently important than to be enrolled among his subjects? For the eternal truth of which he speaks is not abstract but living; he who is himself the truth says to his followers, "Because I live, you will live also" (John 14: 19).

Again, readers of the resurrection narratives might feel that those disciples who saw the risen Christ had an advantage over their fellow-believers of later days. But the risen Christ himself gives the assurance that the advantage, if any, lies with those of later days: "Blessed are those who have not seen and yet have believed" (John

20: 29). And immediately after relating this last beatitude the evangelist tells his readers that the awakening of such belief in them is the purpose of his Gospel. "Jesus did many other signs in the presence of the disciples, which are not written in this book; but these are written that you may believe that Jesus is the Christ, the Son of God, and that believing you may have life in his name" (John 20: 30f).

Epilogue

IT WAS SUGGESTED IN OUR PROLOGUE THAT EVEN A VERY CURSORY acquaintance with the New Testament writings is sufficient to reveal that they all bear consentient witness that Jesus Christ is Lord. That this is so should be abundantly evident now. To all the New Testament writers he is Lord, exalted by God to a position of supremacy over the universe. Even those who record his earthly ministry record it from what is called a "post-Easter perspective", emphasizing as they do so that the exalted Lord is identical with the historical Jesus.

In the earliest days of the apostolic preaching to Israel he was proclaimed as the Messiah, although this was not a claim which he had made for himself in his public ministry. His resurrection, the apostles affirmed, demonstrated him to be Israel's Messiah, the Lord's Anointed, and they strengthened their affirmation by an appeal to those prophetic scriptures which showed "that the Christ should suffer and on the third day rise from the dead" (Luke 24: 46). If he was the Messiah, he was the one addressed by God as "my son" in Psalm 2: 7 and designated "lord" in another psalm (Psalm 110: 1). That the confession "Jesus is Lord" goes back beyond the Gentile mission to the Aramaic-speaking church is indicated by the place secured by the invocation *Marana-tha* ("Our Lord, come!") in the worship of the early church (I Cor. 16: 22; Didache 10: 6).

Christ, Lord, Son of God

When the message of Jesus was carried into the Gentile world, the designation "Messiah" did not have the same relevance as it had for Jews, and Christ (the Greek equivalent of Messiah) came more and

112

more to be used as a personal name and no longer as a title. But its synonyms "Son of God" and "Lord" not only retained but enhanced their relevance. "No one can say 'Jesus is Lord' except by the Holy Spirit", Paul declares (I Cor. 12: 3); John, for whom "Christ" remains a title alongside "Son of God", assures his readers that "every one who believes that Jesus is the Christ is a child of God" and that the world-overcomer is "he who believes that Jesus is the Son of God" (I John 5: 1, 5).[1]

The title "Son of God" bore witness to Jesus' divine being, and so did the title "Lord". Repeatedly the latter title is accorded to Jesus in Old Testament quotations where the primary reference is to Yahweh. If Paul says (perhaps quoting a pre-Pauline confession) that God's purpose is "that at the name of Jesus every knee should bow . . . and every tongue confess that Jesus Christ is Lord" (Phil. 2: 10f), his words echo Isa. 45: 23, where Yahweh says, "To me every knee shall bow, every tongue shall swear". The title "Lord" given to Jesus is "the name which is above every name" (Phil. 2: 9) because it is, in effect, the ineffable name of him who says, "I am the LORD, that is my name; my glory I give to no other" (Isa. 42: 8). But when this name, with the honour due to it, is given to Jesus, it does not detract from "the glory of God the Father"; it augments it (Phil. 2: 11). Similarly, when the readers of I Peter 3: 15 are enjoined, "in your hearts reverence Christ as Lord", the injunction is adapted from Isa. 8: 13, "the LORD of hosts, him you shall reverence". The other leading New Testament writers bear the same witness: "Jesus Christ . . . is Lord of all" (Acts 10: 36); in Heb. 1: 10 he is the one addressed by God himself in the Greek version of Psalm 102: 25, "Thou, Lord, didst found the earth in the beginning . . ."; James calls him "the Lord of glory" (Jas. 2: 1), while in Rev. 19: 16 he is called "King of kings and Lord of lords" (cf. 17: 14).

The Note of Fulfilment

Again, the New Testament message insists that in Jesus and the new order introduced by him the Old Testament has been fulfilled. Over the whole New Testament might be inscribed Peter's words on

[1] Cf. the juxtaposition in John 20: 31, "that you may believe that Jesus is the Christ, the Son of God".

113

the day of Pentecost: "This is that which was spoken by the prophet" (Acts 2: 16). "For all the promises of God", says Paul, "find their Yes in him" – that is, in Christ (II Cor. 1: 20). Or, if I may quote words which I have used elsewhere:

> In Jesus the promise is confirmed, the covenant is renewed, the prophecies are fulfilled, the law is vindicated, salvation is brought near, sacred history has reached its climax, the perfect sacrifice has been offered and accepted, the great priest over the household of God has taken his seat at God's right hand, the Prophet like Moses has been raised up, the Son of David reigns, the kingdom of God has been inaugurated, the Son of Man has received dominion from the Ancient of Days, the Servant of the Lord, having been smitten to death for his people's transgression and borne the sin of many, has accomplished the divine purpose, has seen light after the travail of his soul and is now exalted and extolled and made very high.[2]

The Way of Salvation

One of the aspects of the ministry of Jesus most emphasized as a fulfilment of prophecy is his saving work: "To him all the prophets bear witness that every one who believes in him receives forgiveness of sins through his name" (Acts 10: 43). It is in him that "the grace of God has appeared for the salvation of all men" (Titus 2: 11). "Salvation" is a comprehensive term, embracing many forms of well-being. It may denote political independence, as in Zechariah's hymn, "salvation from our enemies, and from the hand of all who hate us" (Luke 1: 71). But its central New Testament significance appears later in the same hymn, where the newly born prophet goes before the Lord "to give knowledge of salvation to his people in the forgiveness of their sins" (Luke 1: 77). Sometimes it is presented in terms of Christ's victory over hostile forces, among which sin and death are pre-eminent. At a deeper level, it is portrayed as the effect of his self-sacrificing love, by which he absorbed in himself the deadly entail of man's sin and alienation, thus liberating from that entail those who, now united by faith to him, are incorporated in the new humanity of which the risen Lord is the head. However the "great salvation" be conceived – that salvation which "was declared at first

[2] *This is That* (The Paternoster Press, 1968), p. 21.

by the Lord" and attested to others "by those who heard him" (Heb. 2: 3) – it is appropriated by faith. This saving faith is not simply a mental assent to propositions, such as demons can exercise, as James says, without deriving any advantage from it (Jas. 2: 19); it is a personal commitment which issues in action – "faith working through love", as Paul puts it (Gal. 5: 6). The Jesus of the Gospels exults when he finds such faith and cannot withhold any blessing when it is manifested (cf. Matt. 8: 10, 13; 15: 28); so the pervasive New Testament call to faith is summed up in Eph. 2: 8–10: "For by grace you have been saved through faith; and this is not your own doing, it is the gift of God – not because of works, lest any man should boast. For we are his workmanship, created in Christ Jesus for good works, which God prepared beforehand, that we should walk in them." First among these "good works" is love – that love which responds to the love of God and constitutes the fulfilment of his law.

Christ Jesus our Hope

While the distinctive New Testament note is that of fulfilment, the note of hope is present also. The new order inaugurated by Jesus in his death and resurrection is yet to be consummated; his people live "between the times". Here and now they enjoy eternal life, the life of the age to come, because by faith they participate in Jesus' risen life; the power which raised him from the dead is the power that works in their lives. But so long as they live in mortal body, tied to the conditions of earthly existence, they are conscious of a tension between the "already" and the "not yet"; they look forward to the day when "the mortal puts on immortality" (I Cor. 15: 54). But it is not for their own benefit alone that they look forward to that day; that is the day when God's salvation will be perfected, "because the creation itself will be set free from its bondage to decay and obtain the glorious liberty of the children of God" (Rom. 8: 21). This is the new creation, the new heaven and earth of which the prophet spoke, and which John saw realized in his apocalyptic vision.[3]

This new creation in its fulness has not appeared yet, but the Creator Spirit is present and active in the world in general and

[3] See p. 87.

especially in the people of Christ, not only to make effective in them now the deliverance which he effected for them in death and resurrection but to reproduce his love in their lives and enable them to anticipate in actual experience the heritage of glory which lies ahead. "He who has prepared us for this very thing is God, who has given us the Spirit as a guarantee" (II Cor. 5: 5). And it is by the Spirit's operation that the people of Christ, instead of being left as isolated individuals, are united not only to him but one to another, to form the reconciled community which, in God's eternal purpose, is the model for the reconciled universe. This is readily recognized as a leading theme of the letter to the Ephesians,[4] but we may consider whether the same essential insight is not also expressed by James: "Of his own will he brought us forth by the word of truth that we should be a kind of first fruits of his creatures" (Jas. 1: 18). It was in Christ that this purpose of divine love was conceived before the first creation came into being; it was by Christ that its fulfilment was secured when, in the fulness of time, he accomplished his redemptive work, and it is in Christ that it will be realized. He who is our righteousness and our peace is also our hope: this too is the message of the New Testament.

[4] See pp. 40ff.

Bibliography

CULLMANN, O., *The New Testament*, E.T. (London: SCM Press, 1968).

DAVIES, W. D., *Invitation to the New Testament* (London: Darton, Longman and Todd, 1967).

GUNDRY, R. H., *A Survey of the New Testament* (Exeter: The Paternoster Press, 1970).

HARVEY, A. E., *The New English Bible: Companion to the New Testament* (Oxford University Press/Cambridge University Press, 1970).

HOWLEY, G. C. D. (ed.), *A New Testament Commentary* (London: Pickering and Inglis, 1969).

HULL, E., *The Message of the New Testament* (Oxford: Religious Education Press, 1971).

HUNTER, A. M., *Introducing the New Testament* (London: SCM Press, revised edition 1972).

JEREMIAS, J., *The Central Message of the New Testament*, E.T. (London: SCM Press, 1965).

METZGER, B. M., *The New Testament: Its Background, Growth and Content* (London: Lutterworth Press, 1970).

MOULE, C. F. D., *The Birth of the New Testament* (London: A. and C. Black, 1962).

MOULE, C. F. D., *The Phenomenon of the New Testament* (London: SCM Press, 1967).

VAN UNNIK, W. C., *The New Testament: Its History and Message*, E.T. (London: Collins, 1964).

Index

Aaron 77
Abba 19, 29
Abraham 28, 53, 64, 81
Abstinence 45 (see Asceticism)
Access to God 79
Achaia 56
Acts of the Apostles 12, 50ff.
Advent, Second 91, 94f.
Advocate 97
Aegean 100, 101
Allegory 25
Amos 91
Angels, fallen 94
Angel-worship 36
Anointing 98
Antichrist 96
Antinomianism 94
Antioch (Psidian) 60
Antioch (Syrian) 48, 53, 63
Antipas, Herod 20, 55
Apocalypse, Apocalyptic 12, 83ff., 105
Apologists 52
Apostles 62, 68, 71
Apostolic Fathers 53
Aramaic 112
Aratus 54
Areopagus 54
Ascension 38
Asceticism 35, 49
Asia (province) 45, 84ff., 96
Asia Minor 91, 93
Astrology 39
Athens 54
Atonement 76, 97
Augustus 51
Authority 43

Babylonian exile 64
Baptism 35, 38, 60f., 91
Baptism of Jesus 15, 17, 18, 97
Barnabas 57
Barnabas, Letter of 53
Bartimaeus 66
Bath-sheba 65
Beatitude, Last 110f.
Beatitudes 67
Beelzebul 69
Birth, New 117
Bishops 45, 46
Blasphemy 52
Body of Christ 36f., 40
Bread of life 106, 108
Buber, M. 25
Bultmann, R. 27, 39

Caesar 85, 86
Caesarea 50
Caesarea Philippi 19
Calvary 84
Cana 107
Canon 13, 49, 50
Capernaum 18, 59, 108
Capital Epistles 24
Catholicism, Early 43
Centurion 21, 59
Cerinthus 96, 97
Charismatic ministry 43, 44
Charity 33
Children 69f.
Christian 93
Church, churches 36ff., 40f., 43ff., 62, 70, 84ff., 87, 89ff., 92, 116
Church, Household 74
Church order 44ff.
City of God 87
Cleansing 97
Climate of opinion 98, 101
Coleridge, S. T. 41
Colossae 35
Colossians, Letter to 35ff.
Commandment, New 108
Commission of apostles 57, 68, 71
Communion service 16f.
Confession 43, 92
Corinth, Corinthians 16, 24, 25, 45
Corinthians, Letters to 23f.
Cosmic Christ 34ff., 40f.
Cosmic powers 34, 35, 36
Cosmic salvation 40
Covenant 12, 77ff., 87
Creation 34, 36, 54, 75, 96, 103, 104, 106, 116
Creation, New 26, 106, 115, 116
Credal affirmations 48
Cross, crucifixion 16, 17, 19, 21, 22, 28, 52, 55, 86f., 97, 109, 110
Cullmann, O. 86, 117
Curse 28

Damascus road 27, 32
Daniel 18, 84
David 60, 64
Davies, W. D. 117
Deacons 45
Death with Christ 36, 38, 47
Debtors, Parable of Two 30

Dehistoricizing 96, 101
Demons, demonic forces 18, 39, 66
Deposit 46
Diaspora, dispersion 90, 91
Discipleship 68
Discourses, Johannine 107ff.
Discourses, Matthaean 66ff.
Docetism 49, 96f., 101
Dodd, C. H. 20, 108

Easter 25, 53
Egypt 65
Elders 44, 45, 93
Election 87
Elemental spirits 35, 38ff.
Elijah 20, 58
Elisha 58
Emperor-worship 86
Enoch, Book of 83
Entry into Jerusalem 65f.
Ephesians, Letter to 23, 35ff., 40ff., 87, 115, 116
Ephesus 56, 93
Epimenides 54
Epistles (letters) 23ff.
Erskine, T. 31
Eschatology 26, 45f.
Eternal life 96ff.
Ethics 92, 97f.
Eusebius 50, 63
Exhalted Christ 91f., 101, 112

Faith 27, 28, 36, 39, 90, 111, 114f.
Faithful sayings 46ff.
Fate 36, 39
Feeding of multitude 108, 110
Felix 51
Fellowship 69f., 97, 98
Festus 51
Finality of Christ 74ff., 78
Flew, R. N. 31
Flood 94f.
Food 45, 59
Forgiveness 114
Fornication 37
Freedom 32f.
Fulfilment 113f., 115f.

Gadarene demoniac 63
Galatians, Letter to 23, 24, 25, 27ff., 67
Galilee, Galilaeans 17, 18, 25, 55, 58, 62, 63, 68, 70, 71, 102, 110

Galilee, Lake of 65
Gallio 56
Gamaliel 27
Gasque, W. W. 49
Genealogy 64, 65
General (catholic) letters 89ff.
Gentiles, Gentile Christianity, Gentile mission 23, 24, 40, 41, 48, 53, 56ff., 63, 65, 73, 100
Glory 38, 90, 105, 107, 109, 115f.
Gnostics, Gnosticism 45, 49, 96, 98, 101
God, Nature of 54
Golgotha 109
Good Friday 25
Gospel, Gospels 12, 15, 44, 46, 47
Grace 29ff.
Greeks 54
Gundry, R. H. 49, 117

Hagar and Sarah, Allegory of 25
Harvey, A. E. 117
Head (spiritual) 37
Heaven and earth, New 87, 95, 115
Heavenly book 84
Hebrews, Letter to 35, 53, 73ff., 105, 113
Hellenists 48, 53
Herod 51, 64
Historians 50
Historical Jesus 27, 96ff.
History 101
Holiness 92
Holy Land 53
Hope 45f., 115f.
Hosanna 66
House of God 79
Howley, G. C. D. 117
Hull, J. H. E. 9, 60, 117
Humanity, New 114
Hunter, A. M. 117

Idolatry 37
Incarnation 96, 102, 105
Initiation 35
Intercession 75f., 106
Irenaeus 96
Isaiah 69
Isaiah, Book of 15, 20f., 57, 59, 78
Israel 87

James, Letter of 90f., 113, 116
Jeconiah (Jehoiachin) 64
Jeremias, J. 30, 117
Jerusalem 17, 18, 20, 25, 53, 55, 56, 63, 64, 65, 70, 100, 101, 102, 109, 110
Jerusalem, New 87
Jewish Christianity 100
John (Baptist) 15, 17, 18, 20, 51, 57, 58, 109f.
John (Evangelist) 113
John, Gospel of 35, 64, 65, 98, 100ff.
John, Letters of 76, 89, 95ff.

John (Seer) 83ff.
Joseph (husband of Mary) 64, 107
Joseph (patriarch) 53
Jubilee 58
Judaea 17, 102, 110
Judaism 74, 80
Judaizing 45
Judas Iscariot 20
Jude, Letter of 93f.
Judgment 30, 54, 58, 61, 104, 109
Justification 29ff., 32, 48
Justin Martyr 49, 103

Kähler, M. 17
Käsemann, E. 32
Kidron 109
King of the Jews 64, 102, 110
Kingdom of God (heaven) 18f., 25, 61, 66ff., 85
Kingsbury, J. D. 69
Kingship of Jesus 64ff.
Knowledge 98
Knox, R. A. 96

Lamb 84, 85, 87, 106
Last days 61
Last Supper 12, 75
Law, Jewish 25, 27, 28, 29, 32, 35, 40, 45
Law, Roman 25, 55f., 74
Lazarus 107
Letters (Epistles) 12, 13 *et passim*
Letters to Seven Churches 84f.
Leviathan 86
Levitical ritual 74
Life (eternal) 11, 96ff., 106, 111
Light 35, 106, 110
Liturgical ascriptions 48
Logos 103
Lord (title of Christ) 13, 112f.
Lord's Prayer 67f., 71
Lord's Supper 37
Love 68, 97f., 108f., 115
Lowell, J. R. 82
Luke, Gospel of 13, 17, 50ff., 63, 64, 66
Luther, M. 33, 90

Mackay, J. A. 41
Magi 64f.
Majority (spiritual) 29
Manna 108
Manson, T. W. 21, 30, 68
Manuals of instruction 62f.
Marana-tha 112
Mark. Gospel of 13, 14, 15ff., 63, 65, 70, 101, 108
Marriage 45
Martin, R. P. 49
Matthew, Gospel of 12, 62ff.
Melchizedek 75
Messiah, Messiahship 19, 21, 27, 28, 29, 32, 52, 55, 60, 75, 84, 112
Messianic secret 21
Metzger, B. M. 117
Milk (spiritual) 91

Ministry 43ff.
Moses 53, 75, 105
Moule, C. F. D. 117
Mystery, mysteries 35, 42, 48

Naaman 58
Nathan (son of David) 64
Nathanael 64
Nazarenes 32
Nazareth 57, 58, 60, 101
Neill, S. 43
Nero 19, 56
New Testament 12ff. *et passim*
Nicodemus 107
Noah 94

Obedience 98
Old Testament 12, 38, 53, 55, 65, 75ff., 91, 94f., 103f., 113, 114
Olive tree, Parable of 24
Olivet discourse 70
Oral tradition 62
Origen 19

Palestine 17, 23, 101
Papias 63
Parables 24f., 29ff., 68f.
Paraclete 109
Pardon 97
Passion narrative 17, 20f.
Pastoral Letters 43ff.
Patmos 85
Paul 13, 14, 15, 16, 23ff., 32, 44, 53, 54ff., 59, 67, 76, 79, 90, 93, 95, 97, 100, 105, 113, 114, 115
Pentecost 53, 60f., 74
Perfection 35
Persecution 19f., 73, 84ff., 92f.
Person of Christ 75, 95f.
Perspective, Change of 25ff.
Peter 16, 17, 19, 70, 75, 79, 113f.
Peter, First Letter of 91ff., 113
Peter, Second Letter of 13, 93ff.
Pharisee, Pharisees 23, 27, 29, 32, 63, 70
Pharisee and Tax-Collector, Parable of 29
Philippi 56
Phrygia 35
Pierson, A. T. 60
Pilate 55, 64, 102, 109, 110
Planetary powers and spheres 35f., 39
Poor 57, 58f.
Prayer, High-priestly 108, 110
Priesthood (of Christ) 75ff.
Priesthood (of Christians) 92
Principalities and powers 38ff.
Prodigal Son, *Parable of* 30, 31
Prophecy, prophets 94, 103
Prophecy (New Testament) 96
Purpose (Divine) 40ff.

Rabbis 62
Rahab 65
Ransom 21, 31, 48
Reconciliation 31, 40, 42, 116
Redaction 16

Redemption 28, 31
Regeneration 48
Restatement 98
Resurrection (general) 96
Resurrection (of Christ) 26, 28, 29, 54, 60, 66, 68, 106, 110, 112, 115
Resurrection (of Christians) 29, 33, 45, 115
Resurrection (with Christ) 36, 38
Resurrection age 26, 27
Revelation, Book of 35, 83ff., 93, 105, 113, 115
Romans, Letter to 24, 26, 29, 31, 32, 36
Rome, Roman Empire 19, 23, 24, 51ff., 73, 84ff., 91, 92, 93
Ruth 65

Sacrifice, sacrifices (spiritual) 77ff., 92
Sadducees 91
Salvation 56ff., 102, 114f.
Samaria, Samaritans 59, 102, 107, 110
Sanctuary (spiritual) 77, 78, 79
Sanhedrin 52
Schweitzer, A. 32
Scriptures 49
Sedition 52, 55
Sermon on Mount 63, 66, 67f., 91
Serpent (of bronze) 106
Servant of God 20f., 57, 78
Shealtiel 64
Short, A. R. 102
Signs 107ff.
Simeon 56
Socrates 103
Sodom 94
Solomon 53, 64, 105

Solomon, Odes of 86
Son of David 66, 114
Son of God 15, 18, 21, 75, 111, 112f.
Son of Man 18ff., 25, 31, 66, 70, 75, 76, 114
Spirit (of God) 26, 29, 31, 33, 38, 40, 42, 45, 48, 60f., 66, 67, 69, 81, 97, 98, 109, 113, 116
Stephen 52f., 76
Stilling of tempest 63
Stone(s), spiritual 92
Succession (of teachers) 46, 63
Suffering 92f.
Synagogue 57, 60, 68, 70, 74, 108
Synoptic Gospels 15ff., 50ff., 62ff., 102, 110

Tabernacle 105 (see Tent-shrine)
Tacitus 85
Talmud 70
Tamar 65
Tatian 38, 49
Tax-collectors 59
Teachers 46
Teaching of Jesus 62ff.
Temple (Jerusalem) 21, 53, 70, 105
Temple (spiritual) 92
Tent-shrine 53 (see Tabernacle)
Test of faith 71
Theophilus 51
Thessalonians, Letters to 24, 86
Thomas 106
Tiberius 51
Timothy 44, 45, 46
Titus 44, 45, 46
Titus 43ff.
Tradition 13, 16, 23, 36, 46, 81, 102

Transfiguration 20
Trial of Jesus 55
Tribute to Caesar 55
Triumph of Christ 36, 84f., 86f., 114
Truth 82, 101ff. 110
Twelve (apostles) 68

Ugaritic texts 86
Union with Christ 36, 39, 114
Union with God 108f.
Universalism 49
Unknown God 54
Unnik, W. C. van 117

Veil of Temple 21
Vineyard, Parable of Labourers in 30

Wall of partition 40
War against Rome 68, 91
Water of life 106, 107
Watts, I. 95, 107
Wesley, C. 97
Wilderness 53, 94, 108
Wisdom 34, 36, 42, 91, 103ff.
Witness 109
Woman 37
Word 103ff.
World, worldliness 89ff., 98
Wrede, W. 21, 32

Yohânan ben Zakkai 62

Zarephath (Widow of) 58
Zealots 90
Zechariah (Book of) 65
Zechariah (father of John the Baptist) 114
Zerubbabel 64